RIGHTS AND
THE LAW

BY DUCHESS HARRIS, JD, PHD

WITH MARTHA LUNDIN

CONTENT CONSULTANT

HEATH FOGG DAVIS, PHD
DIRECTOR, GENDER, SEXUALITY,
AND WOMEN'S STUDIES PROGRAM
TEMPLE UNIVERSITY

BEING
LGBTQ
IN AMERICA

Essential Library

An Imprint of Abdo Publishing | abdobooks.com

ABDOBOOKS.COM

Published by Abdo Publishing, a division of ABDO, PO Box 398166, Minneapolis, Minnesota 55439. Copyright © 2020 by Abdo Consulting Group, Inc. International copyrights reserved in all countries. No part of this book may be reproduced in any form without written permission from the publisher. Essential Library™ is a trademark and logo of Abdo Publishing.

Printed in the United States of America, North Mankato, Minnesota.
012019
092019

THIS BOOK CONTAINS
RECYCLED MATERIALS

Cover Photo: Shutterstock Images
Interior Photos: Rena Schild/Shutterstock Images, 4–5; Eric Gay/AP Images, 9; Ryan R. Fox/Shutterstock Images, 11; Pablo Martinez Monsivais/AP Images, 12; Ljupco Smokovski/Shutterstock Images, 17; AP Images, 19, 52; Chuck Liddy/Raleigh News & Observer/TNS/Newscom, 22; Rawpixel/iStockphoto, 26–27; Atlanta Journal-Constitution/Georgia State University/AP Images, 31; South Agency/iStockphoto, 33; Olivier Douliery/Abaca/Sipa/AP Images, 36–37; Monkey Business Images/Shutterstock Images, 38; Shutterstock Images, 42, 65, 72, 90; Gerald Herbert/AP Images, 44; Alex Menendez/AP Images, 48–49; Tommy Wu/iStockphoto, 55; Daniela Kirsch/NameFace/Sipa USA/AP Images, 58; Light Field Studios/Shutterstock Images, 60–61; Janson George/Shutterstock Images, 66; Lital Israeli/Shutterstock Images, 70–71; Jacquelyn Martin/AP Images, 75; Joe Amon/The Denver Post/Getty Images, 77; David Zalubowski/AP Images, 79; Dragon Images/Shutterstock Images, 82–83; Joe Raedle/Getty Images News/Getty Images, 87; Jahi Chikwendiu/The Washington Post/Getty Images, 93; Andrew Lichtenstein/Corbis News/Getty Images, 97

Editor: Megan Ellis
Series Designer: Melissa Martin

LIBRARY OF CONGRESS CONTROL NUMBER: 2018965867

PUBLISHER'S CATALOGING-IN-PUBLICATION DATA

Names: Harris, Duchess, author | Lundin, Martha, author.
Title: LGBTQ rights and the law / by Duchess Harris and Martha Lundin
Description: Minneapolis, Minnesota : Abdo Publishing, 2020 | Series: Being LGBTQ in America | Includes online resources and index.
Identifiers: ISBN 9781532119064 (lib. bdg.) | ISBN 9781532173240 (ebook)
Subjects: LCSH: LGBTQ people--Juvenile literature. | Social work with sexual minorities--Juvenile literature. | Minorities--Civil rights--United States--Juvenile literature. | Conflict of laws--Same-sex marriage--Juvenile literature.
Classification: DDC 323.3264--dc23

CONTENTS

People held up celebratory signs outside the Supreme Court after they heard the ruling on *Obergefell v. Hodges.*

"A LITTLE MORE PERFECT"

Hundreds of people gathered on the grass outside the Supreme Court in Washington, DC, in June 2015. They waved rainbow flags and posters in the air while waiting in anticipation to hear the opinion of the court. Most of the crowd were part of the lesbian, gay, bisexual, transgender, and queer (LGBTQ) community. The ruling of the Supreme Court in *Obergefell v. Hodges* would decide whether LGBTQ couples across the United States could legally marry. Some of the people standing outside had been with their partners for years. However, couples who lived in the 13 states that banned same-sex marriage did not have the same rights as married couples. The Supreme Court ruling could change that.

News media interns ran out of the building holding thick pamphlets of paper. They handed the pamphlets to their coworkers. The packets of paper held the decision of the court for *Obergefell v. Hodges*. When people realized the Supreme

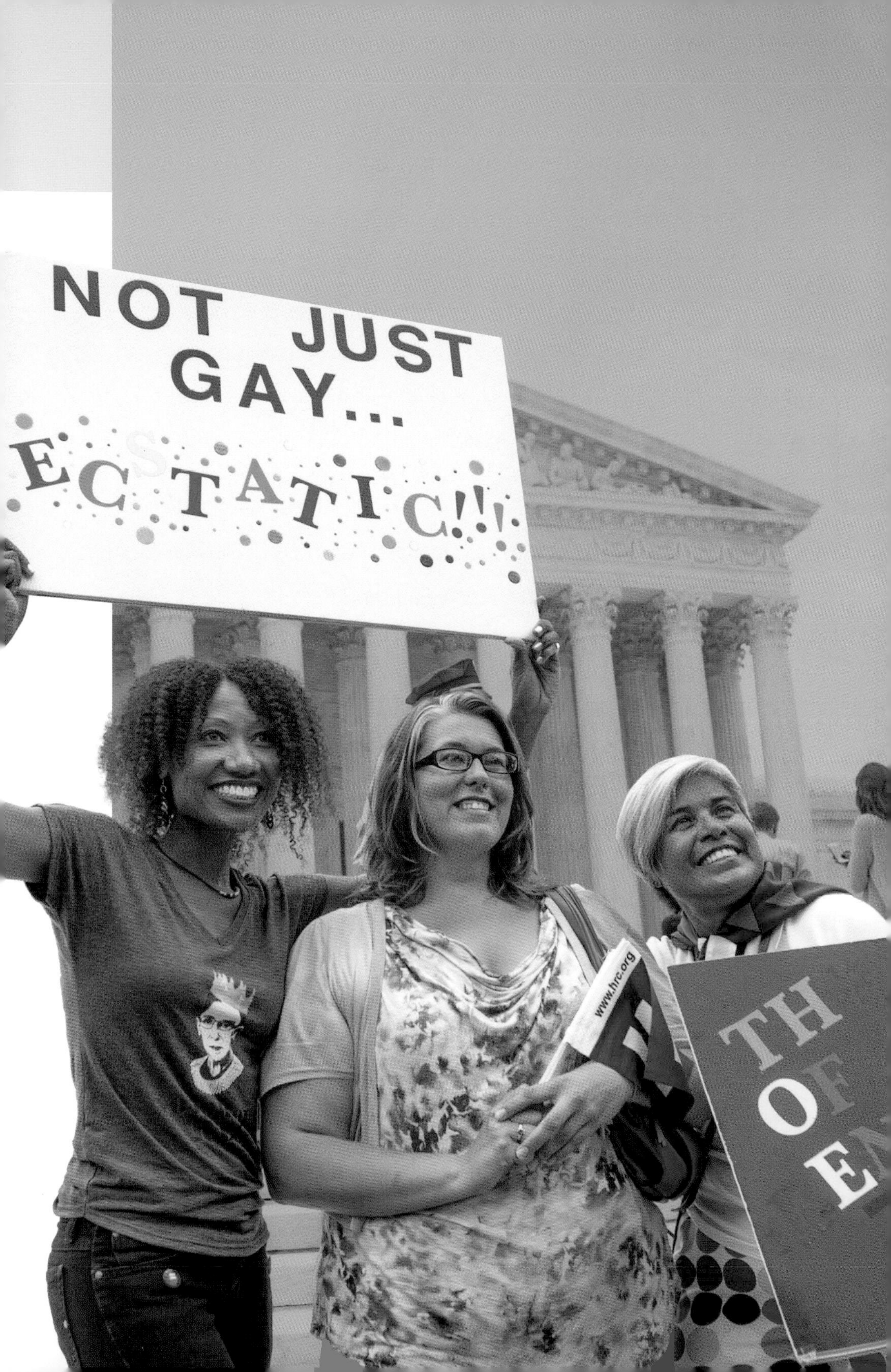
NOT JUST GAY...
ECSTATIC!!!
www.hrc.org

Court had declared that LGBTQ people had the right to marry in the United States, the crowd cheered. Some started to cry from happiness. Reporters from around the country filmed the moment and interviewed people in the crowd. The official opinion of the court was more than 100 pages long. Once the decision was posted on the internet, people read it aloud from their smartphones.

The decision in *Obergefell v. Hodges* protected the right of people to marry a partner of the same sex. It also guaranteed that those marriages would be recognized in every state in the country. That afternoon, President Barack Obama called the ruling "a victory for America." He added, "This decision affirms what millions of Americans already

AN EVOLVING LANGUAGE

Labels are always changing. This is no different in the LGBTQ community. As of 2018, *LGBTQ* was the most current umbrella, or overarching, term for the community. Some people also add *I* for intersex and *A* for asexual. For a long time, the only label used to describe many identities was *homosexual*. Transgender people used to be labeled as *transvestites*, and later as *transsexuals*. Language is always changing, and people can shift labels to best reflect themselves.

Sometimes people reclaim language. *Queer* is one of those words. For many years, *queer* was used as a slur against LGBTQ people. However, some people have chosen to use *queer* as an umbrella term for all LGBTQ people. They may even use *queer* as their own identity, as in the *Q* in LGBTQ. However, not all people feel this way. Some people see *queer* as only a slur. It is important to recognize how language impacts people.

believe in their hearts: When all Americans are treated as equal we are all more free. . . . Today, we can say in no uncertain terms that we've made our union a little more perfect."[1]

However, not every person in the United States agreed with the Supreme Court decision. Chief Justice John Roberts was one of the judges who dissented, or disagreed with the opinion. He didn't think that the Constitution guaranteed marriage equality. In his dissent, he wrote, "Celebrate the opportunity for a new expression of commitment to a partner. . . . But do not celebrate the Constitution. It had nothing to do with it."[2]

Many opponents argued that same-sex marriage went against their religious beliefs. They thought it would go against their freedom of religion guaranteed in the First Amendment. Justice Anthony Kennedy wrote the majority opinion. He said that people were allowed to express their disagreement. However, that didn't mean they could deny marriage equality as a basic civil right.

OBERGEFELL V. HODGES

The landmark Supreme Court case compiled several different petitioners, or parties who wanted the Supreme Court to rule on the issue. In *Obergefell v. Hodges*, four cases—from Ohio, Michigan, Kentucky, and Tennessee—were combined to make the case for the right to marriage equality.

THE OPINION OF THE COURT

Justice Kennedy wrote the majority opinion for the Supreme Court case *Obergefell v. Hodges*. In his opinion, he wrote:

> Far from seeking to devalue marriage, the petitioners seek it for themselves because of their respect—and need—for its privileges and responsibilities. And their immutable nature dictates that same-sex marriage is their only real path to this profound commitment.[3]

In 2018, Kennedy announced his retirement from the Supreme Court. At 81, he was the second-oldest justice sitting on the bench, after Justice Ruth Bader Ginsburg. His retirement left a seat open for President Donald Trump to appoint a new justice. Kennedy was a key swing vote in a number of cases. A swing vote tips the scale one way or another. Kennedy leaned neither liberal nor conservative. He balanced out other justices on the bench. In many recent LGBTQ rights cases, Kennedy wrote the opinion of the court. Kennedy's replacement, Brett Kavanaugh, was confirmed in October 2018. Unlike Kennedy, Kavanaugh is viewed as being very conservative. LGBTQ rights activists worry that the Supreme Court is no longer nonpartisan. They believe that the Supreme Court may not rule in favor of LGBTQ rights in the future.

The combined case is named for Jim Obergefell. Obergefell and his partner of 20 years, John Arthur, were married in Maryland in 2013. They lived in Ohio. Arthur had ALS, which is a degenerative disease that affected his muscle control. Three months after the two men married, Arthur died. Obergefell is listed as Arthur's surviving spouse on his death certificate. At the time, the state of Ohio did not allow same-sex marriage, so it did not recognize the marriage between Arthur and Obergefell. Ohio appealed the decision to include Obergefell's name on the death certificate. It said it would reissue the death certificate without Obergefell's name. Obergefell sued the state of Ohio in 2013. In 2015, his suit became one of the

Jim Obergefell often spoke at events and rallies that supported the fight for same-sex marriage.

cases presented to the Supreme Court. After the federal case took Obergefell's name, the Human Rights Campaign (HRC), one of the nation's largest LGBTQ rights organizations, hired Obergefell to speak about marriage equality across the country.

When the Supreme Court decided to hear arguments, the case was narrowed to two major questions. The first asked: Are states required to license a marriage between two people of the same sex? The other was: Do states need to recognize a marriage that was licensed and performed in a different state? Both of these questions focused on the due process and equal protection clauses of the Fourteenth Amendment to the US Constitution.

The Fourteenth Amendment was one of the three amendments created after the American Civil War (1861–1865). These amendments are also known as the Reconstruction Amendments because they were designed to give citizenship

FOURTEENTH AMENDMENT

When the Fourteenth Amendment was ratified in 1868, it was intended to protect African Americans after the Civil War. However, because of its broad language, its equal protection and due process clauses have been used in cases more than any other amendment. Historically, the Fourteenth Amendment has been used in Supreme Court cases involving many major civil rights issues, including ending segregation (*Brown v. Board of Education*), legalizing interracial marriage (*Loving v. Virginia*), and legalizing early-term abortions (*Roe v. Wade*).

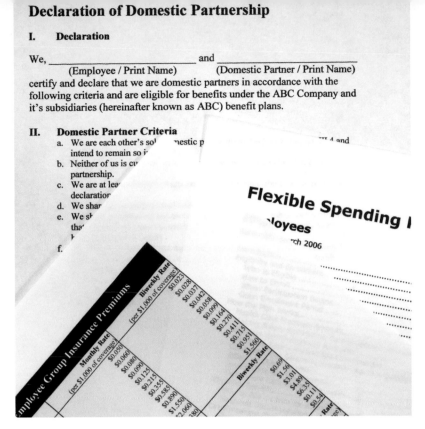

Some same-sex couples opted to get domestic partnerships when marriage was not available. However, these partnerships did not transfer if the couple moved to another state.

in the United States to formerly enslaved black people. The due process and equal protection clauses were important in establishing the rights of African Americans in the 1800s. The due process clause states that no person may be denied "life, liberty or property" without a trial.[4] The equal protection clause is used to protect people from discrimination by the states. This means that all people get certain rights. It ensures that people are treated equally under the law.

Fifteen other couples were listed as the petitioners in addition to Obergefell. Two lawyers, Mary L. Bonauto and

The Supreme Court justices in 2015 were, *left to right*, Clarence Thomas, Sonia Sotomayor, Antonin Scalia, Stephen Breyer, John Roberts, Samuel Alito Jr., Anthony M. Kennedy, Elena Kagan, and Ruth Bader Ginsburg.

Solicitor General Donald Verrilli Jr., argued on their behalf. They needed to show how the equal protection clause could be interpreted to allow same-sex couples to marry. Bonauto and Verrilli argued that same-sex couples were treated unequally in the 13 states that prohibited marriage equality. Some states had passed domestic partnership and civil union laws. But these laws did not grant the full rights, benefits, and protections given to married couples. Any benefits they had were confined to the state they lived in. If a couple moved to a state that did not recognize civil unions or domestic partnerships, those benefits disappeared. Lawyers argued that this could be seen as demeaning and hurtful. This hurt was not only emotional.

It was also harmful in terms of the social benefits the couples were denied.

The respondents, the people arguing that the Constitution did not guarantee the right to marry, argued that marriage equality would fundamentally change the definition of marriage. Lawyers argued that marriage could only exist as a union between one man and one woman. Respondents used history as a precedent. They claimed that same-sex marriage had not existed anywhere in the world until 2001 when the Netherlands became the first country to legalize same-sex marriage. Further, lawyers argued each individual state should decide its own laws regarding same-sex marriage.

Verrilli argued on behalf of the petitioners. In the opening statements he said that if the Supreme Court did not rule, it would be saying that, "the

1,138 REASONS

The Defense of Marriage Act (DOMA) was enacted in 1996. It defined marriage as a union between one man and one woman. Only these married people legally could be called "spouses." The federal government did not have to recognize same-sex couples that were married. DOMA was overturned in 2013. This allowed all same-sex couples to receive the same federal benefits as heterosexual couples. There are 1,138 federal benefits for married couples.[5] Some are very obscure and don't apply to typical married couples, but others are crucial for many families. They include things like filing jointly on taxes, receiving a deceased spouse's retirement benefits, accessing employer-provided health care, and receiving benefits as a veteran's spouse. All of these things are impossible without the label of "spouse."

demeaning, second-class status that gay and lesbian couples now inhabit in States that do not provide for marriage is consistent with the equal protection of the laws. That is not a wait-and-see. That is a validation."[6] Justice Kennedy echoed this in his opinion. He wrote, "There have been referenda, legislative debates, and grassroots campaigns, as well as countless studies, papers, books, and other popular and scholarly writings. There has been extensive litigation in state and federal courts."[7] It was time to make a decision.

MORE THAN A SYMBOL

There are many benefits that go along with attaining a marriage license and saying "I do." For example, the Internal Revenue Service (IRS) considers a married couple as a single taxpayer. This comes with tax deductions. People pay less money in taxes as a couple than if they file taxes individually. And if a partner dies, the spouse is entitled to their partner's Social Security benefits. Spouses can also be listed as next of kin, so a partner can visit and make medical decisions on behalf of their spouse in the event of a medical emergency.

As of 2017, it was estimated that approximately 61 percent of LGBTQ couples were married. This rose from 38 percent before the *Obergefell v. Hodges* decision.[8] Similarly to their heterosexual peers, approximately seven out of ten LGBTQ couples said companionship was a very important reason to get married. However, according to the Pew Research Center, LGBTQ people were "twice as likely as those in the general public to cite legal rights and benefits as a very important reason for getting married."[9]

There is much debate in the United States surrounding the impact of marriage equality. The Supreme Court's decision to legalize same-sex marriage has repercussions in many aspects of LGBTQ people's lives. According to an article in the *Washington Post*, many supporters of marriage equality saw the decision as the "largest conferral of rights on LGBTQ people in the history of [the] country."[10] However, the fight for equal protection and freedom from discrimination is not over. From "bathroom bills," to the right to make a family, to eligibility for military service, there are many rights and laws that continue to challenge LGBTQ people in America.

DISCUSSION STARTERS

- What type of labels do you use to describe yourself? How are those labels similar to or different from the labels other people use for you?

- Can you think of someone in your life, or in the news, whose life was changed by the *Obergefell v. Hodges* decision? How do you think they reacted to the decision?

- Take a look again at Justice Roberts's claim that "the Constitution had nothing to do with [the decision]." What do you think he meant by that? Do you agree with him? Why or why not?

2

WORKPLACE DISCRIMINATION

Employment discrimination has been a problem for LGBTQ employees. While there is not a universal, legal nondiscrimination policy for LGBTQ employees in the United States, many companies now have their own nondiscrimination policies for sexuality or gender identity. As of 2017, 67 percent of the US public supported employment nondiscrimination protections for LGBTQ people.[1] However, this was not always the case.

WORLD WAR II AND McCARTHYISM

After the end of World War II (1939–1945), thousands of soldiers returned home to their families. For many US citizens, the 1950s were a time of reinforcing traditional gender roles. For example, many women who had worked in factories during World War II left their jobs and returned home.

INVESTIGATING COMMUNISTS

The House Un-American Activities Committee (HUAC) began in 1938 as suspicions arose that communists had infiltrated the Depression-era New Deal programs established by President Franklin D. Roosevelt. Many of the programs in the New Deal dealt with unemployment and welfare. HUAC was a committee of US representatives that investigated suspected communists and communist activity. The committee forced people to testify at hearings in front of Congress. HUAC pressured suspects to give information that would lead to further arrests of communists and Soviet loyalists. People who did not testify or give up information could be thrown into prison. Techniques used in the hearings became a model for Senator McCarthy's own hearings about the threat of communism.

Additionally, there was a severe fear of communism coming to the United States. Communism is a political system in which the government controls the means of production. The Soviet Union, which had been an ally of the United States during World War II, became a rival afterward because it was a communist nation.

People thought communism would destroy the United States. This distrust grew into the Cold War (1945–1991). In 1950, hearings began for people suspected of being communists. This period of US history is sometimes called the McCarthy era, after Senator Joseph McCarthy.

Joseph McCarthy was an attorney from Wisconsin. He was elected to the US Senate in 1946 and reelected in 1952.

Senator McCarthy was censured, or condemned, by the US Senate in 1954 as a result of the Red Scare. However, his supporters awarded him a plaque for his "fearless persistence" in battling communism.

Senator McCarthy used the public's fears about the spread of communism in Eastern Europe and China to justify his own search for communists in the US government.

McCarthyism made people distrust those who were different. Celebrities and organizations were blacklisted, which meant they were added to a list of suspected communists. They had a harder time finding jobs because people did not want to associate with communists. The fear of communism was greatest in the federal government. Officials thought communist spies were going to steal government secrets and sell them to Russia. McCarthy's hearings of suspected communists, and the United States' resulting fear of communism, became known as the Red Scare. People often

COMMUNISM IN GAY AND LESBIAN SOCIETIES

The Mattachine Society was founded in 1950 by Harry Hay in San Francisco, California. Hay had been a member of the Communist Party for more than 20 years. In 1951, the Mattachine Society began holding discussion groups. The group was important for building a community of gay men in San Francisco. It allowed gay men to express themselves and live openly. As the group grew, it became politically motivated. However, McCarthyism was at its peak by 1953. In March of that year, a local newspaper noted that Mattachine's lawyer had appeared before HUAC. Afraid of being found to be communist by the government, the leaders of the Mattachine Society stepped down.

referred to communists as "Reds" because of the colors of the Soviet flag.

During the McCarthy era, doctors believed that people with mental illness were more susceptible to communist views. At the time, people viewed homosexuality as a psychological disorder. The government believed that gay and lesbian employees either were communist simply for being gay or were at a higher risk of being blackmailed by communist sympathizers. Because of this, gay and lesbian employees were seen by government officials as a security risk. Hearings began in the late 1940s, targeting suspected communist, gay, and lesbian employees. These hearings, and the subsequent firing of lesbian and gay employees, became known as the Lavender Scare. Lavender was a color historically associated with gays and lesbians. According to an article in *Prologue Magazine*, historians estimate that somewhere "between 5,000 and tens of thousands" of employees were fired from federal positions in the government because they were perceived by others as being gay.[2]

THE BATHROOM BATTLE

As of 2018, there are no federal protections against employment discrimination for LGBTQ people. State governments have their own nondiscrimination policies, but those vary. Some states have no protections for LGBTQ employees. Others have protections only for sexual orientation, not for gender identity or gender expression—the way a person dresses and acts. These policies do more than simply protect an LGBTQ employee from being fired. They impact things as basic as which bathroom an employee can use.

In North Carolina, lawmakers passed House Bill 2 (HB2) in 2016. The media referred to it as the "bathroom bill" because one element of it was that people must use the bathroom that corresponds with the sex markers on their birth certificates. This directly affected some transgender (trans) people, or people whose gender identity does not match the sex they were assigned at birth. It also affected some cisgender (cis) people, or people whose gender identity matches the sex they were assigned at birth. A wide variety of gender expressions exists in the United States. The law was hard to enforce.

Actress Shakina Nayfack, a trans woman, protested HB2 by using the men's restroom at the Legislative Building in Raleigh, North Carolina.

For example, some trans women could use the women's bathroom without being harassed by officials. However, some cis women whom others perceived as too masculine could be harassed. In addition to the restrictions on bathroom use, the bill also prevented cities and other municipalities from making their own nondiscrimination policies for LGBTQ people. Instead, the state's nondiscrimination policy was the final word, and the policy did not include protections based on a person's sexuality or gender identity.

North Carolina lawmakers stated they were protecting women and girls from male sexual predators who would wear women's clothing to gain access to victims in the women's restroom. However, they presented no evidence that a trans woman had ever assaulted someone in a public restroom. Additionally, cisgender women who may dress in a more masculine fashion can have a hard time using a public restroom. In one video recording that allegedly occurred at the airport in Charlotte, North Carolina, a cis woman was dragged out of the restroom line by police who claimed she looked like a man. HB2 also affected feminine-appearing men who sought to use the men's restroom. Other people in the restroom may think that those men do not belong.

LGBTQ rights activists and allies, as well as businesses that North Carolina relied on for income, pressured the legislature to repeal HB2. In 2017, HB2 was replaced by House Bill 142 (HB142). HB142 no longer restricts trans people from using the bathroom that corresponds with their gender identity, but cities won't

HARASSMENT IN PUBLIC RESTROOMS

The National Center for Transgender Equality (NCTE) conducted a survey in 2015. The survey collected responses from more than 27,000 transgender people in all 50 states as well as Washington, DC, Puerto Rico, American Samoa, Guam, and overseas military bases. The results of the survey found that 59 percent of transgender people avoided using public restrooms. Further, nearly one-third (32 percent) limited the amount they ate or drank in order to avoid restrooms. Twelve percent of respondents reported verbal harassment, and 9 percent reported they had been denied access to a public restroom.[3] The NCTE called on governments and businesses to create more inclusive spaces for trans people. This might include single-stall restrooms or more-inclusive nondiscrimination policies.

PROOF OF DISCRIMINATION

At Southeastern Oklahoma State University, Rachel Tudor became the college's first openly transgender professor. She was hired in 2004 and began transitioning in 2007. In 2009, she applied for tenure but was denied. Tenure is a permanent position at a college or university and often comes with financial benefits. Tudor asked for an explanation from her supervisor but never received one. When a male coworker in a position similar to hers was granted tenure, she filed a discrimination complaint. In 2017, seven years after her complaint was filed, a jury ruled in her favor and awarded her $1.1 million in damages.[5]

be able to make their own nondiscrimination ordinances until 2020, shortly after the next election for governor.

CURRENT PROTECTIONS

In April 2019, the US Supreme Court agreed to hear three cases related to LGBTQ employees experiencing discrimination based on their gender identity or sexual orientation. The cases hinged on whether Title VII of the Civil Rights Act of 1964—which prohibits employment discrimination based on a person's race, color, national origin, sex, or religion—applies to LGBTQ people. Some federal courts have ruled that *sex* in Title VII also refers to gender identity and sexual orientation, but other courts have ruled otherwise. As of April 2019, only 21 states and Washington, DC, had employment nondiscrimination policies that included gender identity and sexual orientation.[4] The Supreme Court ruling would decide whether Title VII would apply to LGBTQ people facing workplace discrimination.

One in ten LGBTQ employees has reported leaving a job because of the work environment. A survey in 2011 revealed that 90 percent of trans people had been harassed at work, and trans people are unemployed at twice the national average.[6] Benefits from providing workplace protections for LGBTQ employees include greater job satisfaction and commitment to the company among LGBTQ employees.

While the federal government had not made any laws protecting LGBTQ employees in the United States as of April 2019, public opinion surrounding LGBTQ issues had shifted. In 2002, only 3 percent of Fortune 500 companies had gender and sexuality–inclusive nondiscrimination policies.[7] In 2017, 92 percent of Fortune 500 companies had nondiscrimination policies related to a person's sexuality. Eighty-two percent additionally included policies related to a person's gender identity.[8] As public opinion shifts, laws surrounding workplace discrimination also shift.

DISCUSSION STARTERS

- Have you ever felt as if someone treated you differently because of the way you dress or the way you talk? What does that feel like?

- Why do you think Senator Joseph McCarthy thought gay or lesbian people were more likely to be communists? Would his claim stand up in today's society? Why or why not?

- Why is it important to have nondiscrimination policies for both gender identity and sexuality?

HEALTH
AND PRIVACY

LGBTQ people's relationship with the medical and legal community has been troubled in the United States for hundreds of years. From laws prohibiting same-sex relationships, to cross-dressing laws, to the medicalization of gender identity and sexuality, LGBTQ people have had to fight for the right not only to live openly but also to have truly private lives.

ANTI-SODOMY LAWS IN THE UNITED STATES

The historical perception of LGBTQ individuals influenced laws and prevented LGBTQ couples from living openly throughout the twentieth century. US laws that prohibit nonprocreative sex, called anti-sodomy laws, are as old as the colonies on what is now the East Coast of the United States. Many colonies adopted the laws from the countries the colonists came from, including

THE HISTORY OF SODOMY AND SODOMITES

The term *sodomy* comes from the Bible story of Sodom and Gomorrah. In the Book of Genesis, people in the towns of Sodom and Gomorrah defied God and lived wicked lives. This angered God, who sent two angels to destroy the cities. When the two angels arrived they met up with a man named Lot. The men of the town yelled to Lot, "Where are the men who came to you tonight? Bring them out to us so that we can have sex with them."[1] The angels blinded the men and destroyed the town. When Lot's nephew Abraham looked down upon the towns the next morning, "he saw dense smoke rising from the land, like smoke from a furnace."[2]

Because of this Bible passage, gay men became known as "sodomites," and their behavior was characterized as wicked and evil. Some Christians used the story of God striking down Sodom and Gomorrah in the Bible to justify laws against LGBTQ people. Some recent Bible scholars, however, believe that the interpretation of the men's actions as homosexuality is false. They argue that it wasn't homosexuality but rather rape that God and the angels were condemning.

Britain, Sweden, and Holland. Because of this, laws surrounding sodomy varied greatly between regions. In the 1600s, some colonists went so far as to send people arrested for sodomy back to Britain to be tried there. Most of these anti-sodomy laws quoted the book of Leviticus from the Bible to provide justification. While anti-sodomy laws apply to all people in theory, they disproportionately affected gay men.

Anti-sodomy laws continued to be enforced in varying degrees in the United States through the 1900s. This was not changed until a Supreme Court decision in 2003. John Lawrence was arrested in his Texas home for having consensual sex with another man because a neighbor called the police. The court found Lawrence guilty of "deviate sexual intercourse" and fined him.[3]

However, Lawrence recognized there was something wrong with being arrested in his home. He decided to appeal, and the case eventually reached the Supreme Court as *Lawrence v. Texas*. Part of the Supreme Court's job was to decide whether to overrule the *Bowers v. Hardwick* case from 1986, which upheld a Georgia anti-sodomy law. The court ruled 6–3 in favor of Lawrence, stating that people had an inherent right to privacy in their homes. The court argued that liberty "presumes an autonomy," and that included relationships.[4] The ruling overturned 13 anti-sodomy laws in states across the country. LGBTQ advocates hailed the decision as an important step forward toward equality in the United States.

GEORGIA ANTI-SODOMY LAWS

In 1982, Michael Hardwick was arrested in Georgia for having consensual sex with another man. He appealed his arrest, stating that his constitutional right to privacy had been violated. The case went all the way to the Supreme Court in 1986. On June 30, 1986, the Supreme Court upheld the Georgia statute with a 5–4 ruling in the case *Bowers v. Hardwick*. The court stated that because a majority of people in Georgia believed that homosexual sodomy was immoral, the Georgia statute was constitutional. This ruling was overturned in 2003 as a result of *Lawrence v. Texas*.

PATHOLOGIZING LGBTQ IDENTITIES

In the 1900s, the medical community became the marker for morally acceptable behavior. More and more people looked to science instead of the Bible to know what was acceptable. Society was still influenced by Christian teachings—notably in what was defined as acceptable sexuality. However, there was a shift in the way people talked about sexuality. LGBTQ people, in the eyes of the medical community, had mental disorders. Previously referred to simply as "sodomites," people who were lesbian or gay came to be labeled as "inverts" or were said to have a sexual "perversion."[5]

By the early 1950s, there was a precedent for LGBTQ people to be sent to psychiatric facilities. The first edition of the *Diagnostic and Statistical Manual of Mental Disorders* (*DSM*) was published in 1952. The *DSM* is used by psychologists to diagnose mental illnesses in patients. It listed homosexuality as a treatable disease. These treatments for LGBTQ people included electroshock aversion therapy and lobotomies. One electroshock company said its machine could cure everything from phobias to "transvestites, exhibitionists, alcoholics, shop lifters," and gay identities.[6] While electroshock therapy is no longer endorsed by the American Psychiatric Association (APA) for gay conversion therapy, the method is still utilized by some groups that believe being LGBTQ is a mental disorder.

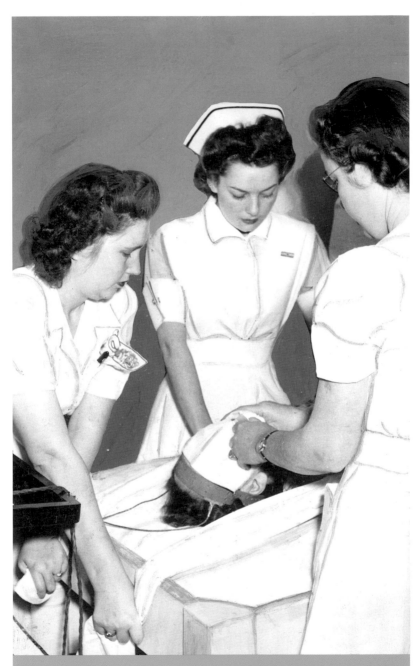

In the 1950s, electroshock therapies were given to some LGBTQ patients. At the time, doctors believed that being LGBTQ was a mental disorder.

THE MEDICALIZATION OF ASEXUAL IDENTITIES

Asexual, or ace, people have no sexual attraction to anyone, or may develop a sexual attraction only after an emotional bond is established. They may be romantically interested in people but have no desire to have sex with them. Many ace-identified people reported feeling broken, assuming they were naturally supposed to want to have sex with people. Some medical professionals made this feeling worse by diagnosing asexual people with a disorder. This leads people in the LGBTQ community to distrust medical professionals. Today, asexuality is becoming more accepted as a sexual orientation. The Asexual Visibility & Education Network (AVEN) has more than 30,000 members.[7] It promotes advocacy and education for asexual people and medical professionals.

Lobotomies gained prominence in the medical field from the 1880s into the mid-1900s. They became a popular procedure for treating various mental illnesses. During what was commonly known as an "ice-pick lobotomy," a thin metal rod was inserted into a patient's brain through the eye socket. A piece of the person's frontal lobe was removed. The frontal lobe is in charge of motor skills, language, memories, and many other things. Lobotomies, though, did not change a person's sexuality. More often than not, there were severely harmful effects. Some of these left the patient unable to speak or perform daily tasks. In the worst cases, the patients died. Doctors discontinued lobotomies as medical treatments in 1954.

The *DSM* listed homosexuality as a psychiatric condition until 1973. It listed gender identity disorder (GID) as a condition until 2013. In 2013, GID was replaced with gender dysphoria. While GID made being transgender a mental illness, gender dysphoria is a condition that describes the stress brought about by having a gender identity that does not match one's biological sex.

People who have gender dysphoria may relieve feelings of anxiety or stress by changing their appearance to reflect their gender identity.

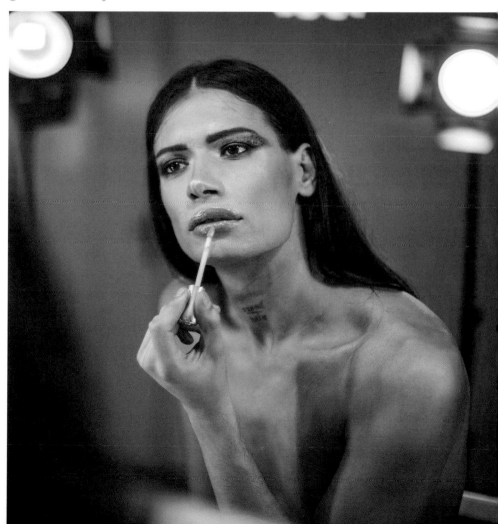

THE INCLUSION OF GENDER DYSPHORIA

Some trans rights activists argue about whether gender dysphoria belongs in the *DSM*. A diagnosis allows trans patients to receive needed care from doctors and mental health care providers. However, it also limits some rights for trans people. Very few insurance policies cover gender-affirming surgeries because they are classified as elective and not medically necessary. People with gender dysphoria have also been excluded from the Americans with Disabilities Act (ADA). Additionally, politicians use the diagnosis as a disorder to keep trans people out of legislation that protects identity groups. Stuck in the middle, trans people receive neither full protection nor care.

VISITATION AND BENEFITS

During a health crisis, hospitals in the United States often have protocols that limit visitors of patients to immediate family only. For LGBTQ couples, that has been historically complicated. Partners of hospitalized loved ones were routinely denied the ability to visit because they were not legally spouses and therefore not considered immediate family.

It wasn't until 2010 that President Barack Obama issued a memorandum charging the Department of Health and Human Services (HHS) with creating guidelines for visitation and medical decision-making for same-sex partners. In 2011, the new regulations went into effect. They granted same-sex couples in civil unions and domestic partnerships visitation rights. Additionally, the guidelines allow patients to make a list of visitors who are allowed in their room, overriding the immediate family rule.

However, there were limits to these guidelines. There have been several instances around the country in which hospital staff have removed partners or not allowed them to enter hospital rooms. These actions can be incredibly aggravating and disheartening for couples who want to spend time with their ill loved ones. When the Supreme Court legalized same-sex marriage in 2015, some of these issues were resolved. But the issue persists for couples who are not married yet or choose to remain unmarried. As the social climate and geography of the country continue to change, so too must the laws to reflect these changing attitudes.

DISCUSSION STARTERS

- Think about something that is really important to you that you don't want other people to see, such as a journal or a text message. How would you feel if someone invaded your privacy and found that item? Why is the right to privacy so important?

- Have you ever visited someone in the hospital, or were you ever in the hospital and someone visited you? Talk about that experience with a friend or adult. What was it like?

- Doctors can't know everything. But we trust them to take care of us. Why might it be a problem if doctors don't understand a patient's medical needs?

4

SAFE SCHOOLS AND STUDENTS' RIGHTS

P olicy making often happens without the input of youth. However, those policies can create environments that are unsafe for LGBTQ students. Bullying and harassment is a problem for many students. But LGBTQ students often have to be their own advocates when administrators are not on their side. Laws are slow to catch up to the rapidly changing environment for LGBTQ-identified students.

ANTI-BULLYING POLICIES

Bullying policies in schools across the United States vary widely and have broad impacts for all students. Many public schools rely on a general policy that protects LGBTQ students in theory but isn't explicit about what counts as bullying or harassment toward those students.

LGBTQ students can experience many types of bullying in school.

Bullying can take many forms, and most don't include physical altercations. Many high school students bully classmates using words. With smartphones and internet access, cyberbullying is becoming more of an issue than ever before. Many anti-bullying policies haven't caught up. However, protections for LGBTQ students are important for the well-being of a school's student population. Anti-bullying policies protect students from being bullied because of their perceived sexual orientation or gender identity. If a male student gets bullied for wearing makeup, these policies ensure the bullies face consequences. If a female student shaves her head and people call her names, she has the school to back her up.

GLSEN is an organization that works to create safe schools for LGBTQ students. Formerly known as the Gay, Lesbian, and Straight Education Network, the group now goes only by GLSEN in an effort to be more inclusive. Its 2015 report, *From Statehouse to Schoolhouse: Anti-Bullying Policy Efforts in U.S. States and School Districts*, found that in states with anti-bullying policies that addressed sexuality, almost 39 percent of public schools did not have protections for students based on sexuality. Sixty percent of public schools in those states did not have protections for students based on gender identity and expression.[1]

GLSEN found that some states had nondiscrimination policy guidelines for school districts to follow. In these states, school districts were ten times more likely to implement policies that protected students based on gender identity and expression. They were also two times as likely to implement protections for students based on sexuality.[2]

CONVERSION THERAPY

Conversion therapy, also known as ex-gay or reparative therapy, seeks to change or "cure" a person's sexual orientation or gender identity. Methods include shaming, hypnosis, and even electroshock treatments. Conversion therapy is widely discredited, and as of 2018, it was banned for minors in 14 states. The APA goes as far as saying that ex-gay therapy is not only ineffective but also harmful, particularly to people under the age of 18. Potential risks include mental illnesses such as depression, anxiety, and self-harming behavior. Research shows that lesbian, gay, and bisexual-identified youth who face rejection from their families are more than eight times more likely to attempt suicide than youth with families who support their sexuality.[5] For transgender and nonbinary youth, that number is even higher. A study done by the American Academy of Pediatrics found more than half of trans boys had attempted suicide. The rates for nonbinary people and trans girls were also extremely high (41.8 percent and 29.9 percent, respectively).[6] Both the American Counseling Association and the National Association of Social Workers are working closely with grassroots organizations and legislators to enact more bans on conversion therapy.

Regardless of anti-bullying policies, many LGBTQ students do not report incidents of bullying. This is for many different reasons. Some students believed that the issue would not be addressed by staff. Others thought it would make the situation worse. More than 60 percent of respondents in the 2011 National School Climate Survey said they did not tell an adult if they were being bullied. Of those who did report incidents, 30 percent reported that nothing was done.[3] A study conducted by the HRC found that LGBTQ students' top two biggest stressors were unsupportive parents and bullying. Non-LGBTQ students' worries were classes, exams, and grades.[4]

Bullying can have destructive consequences. LGBTQ students are five times more likely to attempt suicide than their non-LGBTQ peers, and in 2015, one out of six LGBTQ high school students had seriously considered suicide. The likelihood of self-harm more than doubles among students who are bullied.[7]

However, schools with supportive environments, including expansive anti-bullying policies, showed a safer environment for their LGBTQ students. In 2015, GLSEN conducted the National School Climate Survey. Ninety-seven percent of students in supportive schools could name an adult as an ally.[8] This is important because students are more likely to turn to teachers before school counselors.

TRANS PROTECTIONS IN US SCHOOLS

Access to bathrooms and locker rooms continues to be at the forefront of the legal battle for trans students in school. The question of how to handle trans students feels daunting to many legislators and educators. Some struggle to move past a student's sex assigned at birth. However, these issues go beyond where a trans student should change for gym.

In Virginia in 2018, a transgender student was kept out of the girls' locker room during a lockdown drill. The student, a trans girl, had not been allowed to use any gendered facility such as bathrooms or locker rooms for four years. Teachers didn't know where the student should go during the lockdown drill. She sat in the hallway of the entrance to the locker room. The student wrote a note to the school board. She explained she felt "like an afterthought."[9] The superintendent of the district apologized to the student's mother. However, the

Some schools restrict the bathrooms and locker rooms that trans students can use, which can affect the mental and physical health of the students.

school board has not made any changes to the policies that are currently in place.

Students have begun suing schools for the right to use the bathrooms and locker rooms that correspond with their gender identity. In 2014, the US Department of Education under the Obama administration issued guidelines stating that Title IX, the law which prohibits sex discrimination in education, also protects trans students. Those guidelines have since been revoked during the Trump administration. Further, in 2018, the Department of Education dismissed Title IX complaints on the issue of trans students' right to use the bathrooms that correspond with their gender identity. Liz Hill, a spokesperson for the Department of Education, stated simply, "Title IX prohibits discrimination on the basis of sex, not gender identity."[10]

Many trans students fear that this will expose them to more violence. While US secretary of

BEING LGBTQ IN SCHOOL SPORTS

In a survey conducted in 2011, GLSEN reported its findings on LGBTQ students' involvement in school sports. They found that LGBTQ students are one-half as likely as their straight peers to participate in sports.[11] Even though studies show that LGBTQ students who are also athletes are more likely to have higher self-esteem and a greater sense of belonging at school, LGBTQ students can run into barriers when competing in high school sports. Students reported harassment as well as discrimination from certain teams. For trans and nonbinary students, gender-segregated teams and locker rooms create even more significant barriers.

Under the leadership of Betsy DeVos, *center*, the Department of Education stopped hearing Title IX complaints from trans students in 2018.

education Betsy DeVos stated that it was still a school's job to protect all students, Catherine Lhamon, who worked for the Obama administration as the assistant secretary for civil rights, called the policy change "appalling and deeply dangerous."[12]

The repercussions of incomplete nondiscrimination policies affect LGBTQ students at every level of education. The Climate Survey shows that LGBTQ students were more likely to miss school, have lower grade point averages, and have higher rates of mental illness than their non-LGBTQ peers.

"DON'T SAY GAY" STATES

In the United States, eight states have legislation in place that limits or prohibits educators from either using the word *gay* or teaching about LGBTQ topics in their classrooms. This has serious repercussions not only

CONSEQUENCES FOR LGBTQ TEACHERS

For teachers who choose to ignore "Don't Say Gay" rules, there can be critical consequences. Stacy Bailey, an elementary school art teacher in Texas, was suspended without pay in September 2017 for talking about her wife in class. Some teachers say the laws reflect parents' concerns about discussing sex in school, but many teachers argue that the laws go much further than just talking about sex. "It creates a culture of silence," says Troy Williams, executive director of Equality Utah.[13] Students recognize when teachers are not saying something. It increases the stigma that already surrounds LGBTQ students. One teacher in Utah said that she loses "teaching moments" because she is not able to answer students' questions directly.[14]

THE IMPORTANCE OF GSAs

Some schools can be hostile toward LGBTQ students. However, studies show that having a gay-straight alliance or gender-sexuality alliance (GSA) is an important step in creating a safer school environment. GLSEN, an LGBTQ student advocacy group, does a National School Climate Survey every two years around the country. Its findings conclude that students with access to a GSA report less harassment and miss less school than peers without a GSA. It also found that students who were a part of a GSA were better able to find supportive adults within the school, which has been shown to lead to a higher grade point average.

for students but also for educators who are trying to foster diversity in the classroom.

In Alabama, Arizona, Louisiana, Oklahoma, Mississippi, Texas, South Carolina, and Utah, state laws restrict teachers in what they can and cannot say about LGBTQ topics. In Alabama, teachers are required to state that "homosexuality is not a lifestyle acceptable to the general public and that homosexual conduct is a criminal offense under the laws of the state."[15] The state law this refers to has been unenforceable since *Lawrence v. Texas* in 2003. Other states, such as Arizona, require that curricula not promote homosexuality or even refer to LGBTQ topics positively.

Laws vary from state to state. Some teachers aren't allowed to say the word *gay*. Others have restrictions on images they use. Any images that may be seen as promoting nonheterosexual relationships are not allowed. Many students rely on health teachers to provide a comprehensive education on safer sex practices. However, students in states with a "Don't Say Gay" ban are provided either an abstinence-only education or sex-ed focused on heterosexual relationships only. This type of teaching can have serious consequences for students in opposite-sex relationships, too. Five of the eight "Don't Say Gay" states reported some of the highest rates of teen pregnancy in the United States in 2016.[16]

This sometimes leaves sexual education up to student-led groups such as gay-straight alliances or gender and sexuality alliances, both known as GSAs. For one GSA in Alabama, the club's president says that the meeting that discusses sexual health and education is the best-attended meeting of the year. However, without an expert guide such as a knowledgeable teacher, GSAs can get lost with misinformation.

DISCUSSION STARTERS

- Think about the climate in your own school. What do you think it is like for LGBTQ students?

- Do you know what the anti-bullying and nondiscrimination policies are for your school? Talk to a teacher or a principal to find out. Do they include all students? If not, try to find out why.

- Do your teachers include information about LGBTQ people and issues? If they don't, why do you think that is? Is there something you can do to promote more discussion of these topics in your classes?

5

Protesters gathered after a 2018 memo from the HHS sought to define gender as unchangeable from birth.

LOST IN TRANSLATION

Almost every non-Western culture in the world recognizes people who identify with a third gender or more than one gender. In some cultures, gender-nonconforming people are placed in positions of power and respect. In Iran, where being gay is still punishable by death, trans people have access to gender-affirming surgeries. After surgery, a person's documents are changed. Across southern Asia, men take up the roles and dress of women and have a distinct gender outside of "man" or "woman."

Western civilizations in particular adhere to a binary of male and female with no other options. Sex and gender are often believed to be the same thing. However, scientific understanding is catching up to what people elsewhere in the world have held for centuries.

TRANS IS BEAUTIFUL
EQUALITY FLORIDA
STANDS WITH
#Won't Be Erased!
What good are my rights if my family has none?

NATIVE LANGUAGE RECLAMATION

In the 1990s, Native American LGBTQ activists came up with the term *two-spirit* to describe LGBTQ tribespeople. "Two-spirit" was taken from the Ojibwe label for LGBTQ people.[3] This was meant as an alternative to the Western labels of *gay*, *lesbian*, *bisexual*, and *transgender*. Prior to the creation of the term, many tribes had words to describe gender-variant people. Each tribe had a different word. Navajo called these people *Nádleehí*—meaning one who is transformed. The Crow nation used *Badé*. The Lakota used *Winkté*. For the Cheyenne, these people were called *Hemaneh*. Today, many Native American languages have been lost due to colonization and assimilation of native peoples. In some cases, such as with Cherokee, only 1 percent of Cherokee people are fluent in the language.[4]

Assimilationist practices condemned two-spirit people. In the Crow nation, one Christian minister spent so much time condemning the Badé that Crow elder Thomas Yellow Tail believes that the minister "may be the reason no others took up the Badé role."[5] However, work is being done to bring back the languages, and with it, an understanding and acceptance of two-spirit people. The Cherokee language has ten different pronouns, and all of them are gender neutral.

BIOLOGICAL COMPLEXITIES

Scientists distinguish between several different biological sexes. According to an article in *Scientific American*, "many of us are biological hybrids on a male-female continuum."[1] These biological sexes can vary widely. Typically, an XX chromosome makeup determines a female sex, and an XY makeup determines a male sex. However, there can be females who have XY, and males with XX. There can be people with only one sex chromosome, and others with three (XXY, XYY, XXX). When people have an atypical chromosome makeup or do not exhibit typical genitalia, they are called intersex. This group of people makes up about 1.7 percent of the population.[2] Not all intersex people have atypical sex characteristics. Intersex individuals are sometimes included in the LGBTQ community because of how the medical community treats them. But biological sex and gender identity are two distinct concepts.

In the past, if a child had ambiguous genitalia, the parents made a decision about which sex they'd prefer their child to be. Doctors then performed invasive surgeries on the infants and young children to construct typical sex organs. However, these surgeries are medically unnecessary. Intersex rights advocates say children should be able to decide what is done to their bodies. Medical practices are starting to change. Parents often speak with a team of specialists before considering surgeries. However, there are no consistent laws surrounding infant genital surgery. This means there are wide differences depending on which doctor or surgeon is working.

During puberty, an adolescent's secondary sex characteristics may not be consistent with the gender that was constructed in infancy. Sometimes this causes gender dysphoria and depression. This can lead intersex people to undergo hormone replacement therapy and more surgeries. Further, when intersex individuals reach adulthood, health care providers are often clueless as to their patients' needs. That leaves intersex people responsible for educating doctors in their own care.

IMPACT ON SAFETY

The emphasis on strict sexual binaries has led to a long history of laws about cross-dressing in the United States. As recently as 2011, a man could be arrested in New York for wearing women's clothing. The laws date back to 1848, when an Ohio law made

During World War II, many women entered job fields that had previously only been open to men. These jobs, often in factories, required women to adopt more masculine clothing.

it illegal for a person to appear in public "in a dress not belonging to his or her sex."[6] This law was followed by several others in various states during the 1850s.

Women didn't begin to wear pants in everyday society until World War II, when they were required to take over the jobs typically held by men. It wasn't until the 1960s that lasting change was possible in women's fashion. Still, even as pants became a staple in nearly every closet in America, female US senators were not allowed to wear pantsuits on the Senate floor until 1993. Though some regulations dictating what women could wear were lifted, the same cannot be said for men. Many of the laws enacted in order to prevent cross-dressing for all were amended to exclude only

THREE ARTICLES

In New York City in the mid-1900s, people were required to wear at least three articles of "gender-appropriate" clothing.[7] This meant clothing that matched a person's assigned sex at birth. For drag queens and trans women in the Greenwich Village neighborhood, the three articles rule could be dangerous. Many gender-nonconforming people were arrested for violating the statute against cross-dressing. Police raids on bars where LGBTQ people gathered were common in the 1960s. In 1969, tensions boiled over at the Stonewall Inn. This gay bar was a favorite gathering place for many drag queens and trans women. Instead of going quietly in the police van during a raid, the trans women began to fight back. Eventually, others began to join in. This began a weeklong uprising in Greenwich Village. The uprising sparked a national conversation and launched what is considered today to be the modern LGBTQ rights movement.

men from cross-dressing. Trans women faced more violence because of these amendments.

Trans people of all identities have trouble in the workplace. Even though cross-dressing laws changed, dress codes weren't quick to follow suit. Many butch, or masculine, women as well as trans men were still required to wear dresses or skirts to their jobs. One of these people was Leslie Feinberg. Feinberg was a butch lesbian who lived in Buffalo, New York, in the second half of the twentieth century. Feinberg used the personal pronouns *zie* and *hir* toward the end of Feinberg's life. Feinberg had a masculine appearance and faced a lot of harassment for the way zie looked. Employers were unwilling to hire hir. Feinberg was forced to take many low-paying jobs. In 1993, Feinberg published hir first novel, *Stone Butch Blues*. The novel focused on a young person named Jess who navigated their changing gender and sexuality. It changed the way people saw gender presentation. *Stone Butch Blues* won many awards. It is still regarded as one of the most accurate portrayals of a transgender person in literature.

Trans women, particularly trans women of color, are murdered with alarming frequency in the United States. Many of those deaths go unreported and uninvestigated. It is difficult to know the exact numbers of trans women killed in the United States each year. Tracking statistics is difficult due to the high levels of homelessness among this group. Further, not all deaths

The transgender pride flag has the colors blue, pink, and white.

are reported, while some are reported using a woman's birth name and sex marker—the name and sex marker assigned at birth that is on her state identification document (ID).

Even those few murder cases that do go to trial face another hurdle. Some defendants claim they panicked when they found out the gender identity or sexual orientation of a person. This panic made them unable to think through their actions and led to the person killing a gay or trans person. Colloquially this is known as "gay panic" or "trans panic." Juries are told not to rely on the panic defense to make their decision. But biases that already exist in the jury are hard to overcome. There are no rules outlawing the use of the gay/trans panic defense.

Attorneys continued to use the tool in 2018. The results of such a defense often mean the person is given a lighter sentence, or none at all. LGBTQ victims are left without justice.

GENDER MARKERS

For trans people, it is important that official documents reflect their gender identity. Having IDs that are consistent with a person's identity and presentation can help keep trans people safe from some types of harassment. For example, a trans man may get stopped in an airport. The information on his ID may not match his presentation. This can be humiliating. However, changing a name and gender marker on official documents is a hassle and can be expensive. A court order for a name change can cost anywhere between $150 and $500, depending on the state.[8] Courts may also order people to make an announcement in the local newspaper. This may put trans people at risk by publishing their address. The name change does not impact the gender marker on any documents.

Changing a gender marker on a passport or other official document requires a note from the person's doctor. The doctor must state that the person petitioning for a change in gender marker has undergone or is in the process of undergoing "appropriate clinical treatment."[9] Appropriate clinical treatment can vary from doctor to doctor and may be as simple as seeing a psychologist for depression and anxiety that's often associated with gender dysphoria. It may go as far as requiring gender-affirming surgery.

As of 2018, the only gender markers allowed on a US passport are male or female. However, some states have passed laws allowing for a third nonbinary option on state documents. Many LGBTQ advocates see this as a step in the right direction for trans equality, but some experts are not so sure. Experts in Australia caution that not all countries will allow people with a nonbinary option listed as their sex to enter the country. Still, for those individuals whom "M" or "F" doesn't fit, a third option such as "X" can be important in validating their identities.

Often the system doesn't work in trans people's favor. CeCe McDonald is a black trans woman. She is also an activist and prison system abolitionist. One night in Minneapolis, Minnesota, McDonald was out with

RENEE RICHARDS

Renee Richards is a trans woman and pro tennis player. In 1975, she underwent gender-affirming surgery, and in 1976, she won a tennis tournament in California. She was outed by someone in the crowd. Richards was supposed to compete in the US Open tournament, but the US Open began a chromosome screening process. Their position was that only "women born women" were allowed to play.[10] Richards sued the United States Tennis Association (USTA) for discrimination. USTA lawyer George Gowan claimed that trans athletes had an unfair advantage. The judge, Alfred Ascione, noted that there were very few trans athletes. He argued that if trans women truly had an advantage, more would be playing professional sports. Ascione ordered that Richards be allowed to play in the women's tournament at the US Open.

CeCe McDonald, *right*, and actress Laverne Cox discussed transgender rights during a screening of the documentary *Free CeCe*.

some of her friends. A group of people began harassing her. They threw bottles at her head. She tried to run away but one of the men caught her. McDonald reached into her purse and pulled out a pair of scissors. Her attacker stabbed himself on her scissors. He died. Even though McDonald was defending herself, police still arrested her. She went to a men's prison in Minnesota because her sex marker on her birth certificate was M. This put her in danger of violence and harassment. McDonald was released after 19 months in prison. She now gives lectures around the country about her time in prison. McDonald said, "I have nightmares of walking through prison naked and having people just, like, peer at me." In her activism, McDonald stresses the humanity of trans people. She says, "We have lives. We have people who love us. We need the same opportunities in life to survive and to live and to thrive."[11]

DISCUSSION STARTERS

- Do you think medical schools should better educate doctors to treat intersex people, so intersex patients don't have to educate their doctors? What are some actions doctors can take to address the lack of education about intersex people?

- Do you see a shift in public acceptance of trans people? Explain your answer.

- It is very difficult to be 100 percent masculine or 100 percent feminine. In what ways do you go against gender stereotypes?

LGBTQ service members face many challenges, both legal and personal, to serve in the US military.

LIFE IN
THE MILITARY

L GBTQ people have been serving in the US military for hundreds of years. However, homosexual conduct of any kind has been grounds for punishment and discharge for nearly all of that history. Leading up to the start of World War II, homosexuality was listed as a mental illness. This meant gay men and lesbians could be excluded from enlisting. Military personnel interviewed all people enlisting and could deem people with certain medical conditions unfit. Homosexuality was considered one of these conditions.

The enforcement of these bans on LGBTQ service members ebbed and flowed depending on the time period. During periods of war, particularly during the Vietnam War (1954–1975), many officers turned a blind eye. During World War II, homosexual conduct was often cited as "deprivation" homosexuality—something that could not be avoided due to the stresses of war.[1] But discharges soared after World War II.

WWII VETERAN UNDERGOES GENDER THERAPY

While serving in the US military during World War II, a soldier found an article about a Danish doctor who was pioneering research in gender therapy. Christine Jorgensen, then George, decided to fly to Denmark and meet this doctor in 1950. Jorgensen went through more than a year of hormone treatments under the care of her doctor and then underwent several surgeries to complete her transition. Upon her return to the United States, one newspaper reported her transformation with the headline, "Ex-GI Becomes Blonde Beauty!"[3] Over the next 30 years, Jorgensen found support and success within Hollywood.

LGBTQ people didn't stop serving in the military. They decided instead that they wouldn't talk about their identity. If anyone were to find out, they risked being discharged, losing their veterans benefits, and sometimes experiencing violence. Violence could come not only from the public but also from their own comrades. In 1981, the Department of Defense reaffirmed the ban on gays and lesbians in the armed forces. During the 1980s, the military discharged more than 17,000 service members under the homosexuality category.[2]

DON'T ASK, DON'T TELL

President Bill Clinton said that if he were elected, he would lift the ban on gay people serving in the military. LGBTQ advocates were excited to finally gain some traction in the fight for equality. However, upon entering office in 1993, Clinton was met with strong opposition to lifting the ban. Some opponents believed that gay men and lesbians who served openly would disrupt their units. Others feared violence and the disruption that homophobia might create on a team that relied on cooperation. Further fears had to do with seeing the LGBTQ community as a special interest group, or a group of people who sought political advantages.

A compromise was suggested. At the time, recruits were asked about their sexual orientation upon enlisting. If the question wasn't asked, and nobody talked about

SYMBOLS OF SEXUAL ORIENTATION

Adolf Hitler and the Nazi Party, which controlled Germany before and during World War II, saw gay men as a threat to the goal of expanding the Aryan race. Thousands of gay men were sent to concentration camps along with Jews, Roma, disabled people, and other groups of people. The pink triangle used in the LGBTQ rights movement comes from the Holocaust. Gay men in concentration camps were given uniforms with pink triangles sewn onto their breast pockets. "Antisocial" women, which often included lesbians, were given black triangles. These symbols were used as a way to identify prisoners. When Allied forces liberated concentration camps in 1945, gay men faced an uncertain future. Because homosexuality was still outlawed in Germany and the United States, some gay men were taken from the concentration camps and brought to prisons to serve out the rest of their sentences. Changes in German law that completely decriminalized homosexuality didn't come until 1994.

The pink triangle was forgotten until the early 1970s, when a Florida activist used the symbol to protest against an act that would repeal LGBTQ housing protections. During the AIDS crisis in the 1980s, use of the pink triangle continued to grow. In the 1990s, lesbians began using the black triangle. The triangle is cited by activists as a symbol of solidarity so that "history [would] not repeat itself."[4]

it, LGBTQ people could quietly serve in the military. Consequently, the Don't Ask, Don't Tell (DADT) law was passed in 1993. It was supposed to be a compromise, but there is little evidence that life for LGBTQ service members improved after the passing of DADT.

If a person's sexuality was revealed, that person would still be discharged. However, the nature of that discharge changed with DADT. Prior to the rule, gay men and lesbians were given less than honorable discharges, which often disqualified them from any public sector job and military benefits. However, gay men and lesbians discharged during DADT were often given honorable discharges.

These were minor improvements in the larger context of the military, but there is little evidence suggesting DADT did anything to change the way officers treated soldiers. By 2009, 13,000 service members had been discharged from the

"I AM A HOMOSEXUAL"

In 1975, Air Force Sergeant Leonard Matlovich was on the cover of *Time* magazine. Matlovich was an active-duty service member and was wearing his uniform in the photo. The headline read "I Am A Homosexual."[5] Matlovich was the first openly gay person to be featured on the cover of a news magazine in the United States. After the magazine was published, Matlovich was discharged from the military. He later sued the military and won a retroactive promotion for how he was discharged.

Though President Clinton said he was a supporter of LGBTQ rights before he was elected, DADT was passed during his presidency.

military since DADT went into effect.[6] Harassment was rampant within the ranks. Some harassment was so bad that soldiers came out of the closet just to escape the military. Little was done to curb the harassment. Sailor Lori Smith, who was in the US Navy, said, "I tried to go to the chaplain. I tried to go to the

Current and veteran LGBTQ soldiers march in Pride parades to increase their visibility in society.

lieutenant and tell them that this stuff is going on and all they said was, if there's nothing really physical that's happening to you, there's nothing they can do."[7] Even when harassment did become physical, some say officers looked away. In 1999, Army Private Barry Winchell was beaten to death. Soldiers in the company spread a rumor that he was gay. Two of his barrack mates, Justin Fisher and Calvin Glover, got drunk in the early hours of July 5. At some point in the early morning, Glover took a baseball bat and beat Winchell to death while he slept.

Those who were in the military prior to the repeal of DADT were forced to keep their sexuality a secret. Nathaniel Boehme is the LGBTQ veteran coordinator at the Oregon Department of Veterans' Affairs. He speaks with LGBTQ veterans around the state. He says that few LGBTQ service members want to identify as veterans. He says they "identify much more closely with the LGBTQ community."[8] LGBTQ veterans are less likely to utilize resources through the Veterans' Affairs (VA) office. They don't want to relive the worst years of their lives.

DADT was repealed in 2010. The Don't Ask, Don't Tell Repeal Act came after a survey of the armed forces revealed that 70 percent of military personnel said that lifting DADT would have mixed, positive, or no impact.[9] The repeal was a time for celebration for some service members. However, others felt it was a reminder that they were not able to be out. For transgender service members, the ban on service wasn't lifted

Injuctions on Trump's ban on trans people serving in the military went in place in 2017. This allowed trans people to enlist in the military starting January 1, 2018. However, Sparta, an organization that works with trans troops, recruits, and veterans, said that very few trans people were being accepted. More than 140 of its members tried to enlist, but only a few were accepted.

Then, in January 2019, the Supreme Court ruled that the ban could remain in place while lower court cases challenged the ban. According to Jennifer Levi from GLBTQ Legal Advocates and Defenders, the Supreme Court ruling "means that courageous transgender service members will face discharges while challenges to the ban go forward." Levi added that the ban "defies reason and cannot survive legal review."[10] While the ban remains in place, trans servicepeople are at risk of being discharged due to their gender identity. Additionally, trans people may no longer enlist in the military.

until 2016 by President Barack Obama. Then, in 2017, President Trump issued an executive memo reinstating the ban.

BEING TRANS IN THE MILITARY

At the end of 2017 and into 2018, several developments came in rapid succession regarding the status of trans military members. In 2017, President Trump tweeted that trans people would not be allowed to serve. In a series of tweets, he stated,

> *After consultation with my Generals and military experts,*
> *please be advised that the United States Government will*
> *not accept or allow Transgender individuals to serve in any*

capacity in the U.S. Military. Our military must be focused on decisive and overwhelming victory and cannot be burdened with the tremendous medical costs and disruption that transgender in the military would entail.[11]

In March 2018, the White House issued a report detailing the justification for reinstating the ban on trans people. The report suggested trans soldiers would undermine unit cohesion and impair unit readiness. In 2018, several lower courts put injunctions, or blocks, on the ban after trans soldiers sued the administration for discrimination. However, in January 2019 the US Supreme Court ruled that the ban could remain in effect until cases about it go through federal appeals courts. As of that time, the legality of the ban remained undecided.

DISCUSSION STARTERS

- Some politicians believe that LGBTQ soldiers will disrupt unit cohesion. How do you think they came to this conclusion?

- What qualities do you think people need to have in order to be in the military?

- Do you think a president should announce policy changes on social media? Why or why not?

Achieving marriage equality in all 50 states took many years and several court cases.

THE FIGHT FOR MARRIAGE EQUALITY

Since the 1970s, activists began calling for marriage equality. It has been a huge goal of the LGBTQ rights movement. However, there were many obstacles in the way. Many people believed that marriage should only be between one man and one woman. This was a strongly held belief that still exists today. Marriage equality can be a divisive issue. But equality between married couples is important so that all people receive the same benefits.

DEFENSE OF MARRIAGE ACT

The Defense of Marriage Act (DOMA) was signed into law in 1996. DOMA defined marriage as a union between one man and one woman. DOMA did not directly ban same-sex marriages, but it did deny federal benefits to same-sex couples. By law, the individuals in those couples could not be called "spouses."

Protesters gathered in various states to advocate for marriage equality laws and amendments in the years after DOMA was passed.

Little information exists about the events leading up to the passing of DOMA. The bill was signed into law at 12:50 a.m. on a Saturday morning. President Clinton had just returned from a campaign trip to South Dakota. No photo was taken at the signing. There is no mention of it in Clinton's 1,000-page memoir. In interviews, Clinton has given little insight into why he signed the bill at all. Speculation is all most researchers can gather.

During his campaign, Clinton was the first candidate to openly support LGBTQ rights on a national platform. However, upon entering office, it became increasingly clear that he was ahead of public opinion. In the mid-1990s, support for marriage equality was at only 30 percent.[1] After DADT, the president stepped back from his vocal support of LGBTQ rights. He stated that he did not support marriage equality.

DOMA was passed in Congress with 427 in favor and only 81 opposed between the House and the Senate.[2] Even if Clinton had wanted to veto the bill, Congress had the two-thirds majority necessary to override his veto. While DOMA's passing did not infringe on states' rights to pass their own definitions of marriage, DOMA slowed down the process of marriage equality in the United States.

PRESIDENT CLINTON'S OPINION ON DOMA

In March 2013, shortly before the Defense of Marriage Act (DOMA) was ruled unconstitutional, former president Clinton wrote an op-ed in the *Washington Post* about his feelings about the act and its place in American history.

> *When I signed the bill, I included a statement with the admonition that "enactment of this legislation should not, despite the fierce and at times divisive rhetoric surrounding it, be understood to provide an excuse for discrimination." Reading those words today, I know now that, even worse than providing an excuse for discrimination, the law is itself discriminatory.*[3]

Recognizing mistakes is important. Clinton's change in attitude reflected a growing shift throughout the United States. Based on a Pew Research poll, 2011 was the first year more Americans approved of same-sex marriage than opposed it.[4] Since that time, that number has only grown.

DECISION BY THE STATES

After the passing of DOMA, states began creating their own legislation defining marriage. A string of legislative and statutory bans on same-sex marriage entered ballots across the United States. By 1997, only 16 states did not have laws regarding same-sex marriage.

By 2003, that number dropped to only seven states. But 2003 was a turning point for legislative measures. Massachusetts became the first state to recognize and support same-sex marriages for LGBTQ couples. The next state to recognize same-sex marriages was Connecticut in 2008. In 2013, DOMA was ruled unconstitutional by the US Supreme Court in *United States v. Windsor*. By then, 16 states had legalized same-sex marriages.

EDIE WINDSOR'S CASE

Edie Windsor is a famous early activist in the LGBTQ movement. In the 1960s, she met and fell in love with Thea Spyer, a psychologist. They were engaged for 40 years before marrying in Canada in 2007. Dr. Spyer died in 2009. Windsor inherited Spyer's estate. However, their marriage was not recognized in the state of New York. The IRS sent a bill to Windsor's house. It said she owed more than $300,000 in taxes. If the marriage had been recognized, there wouldn't have been a bill. She appealed, saying that the law against same-sex marriage set up LGBTQ couples for different treatment than their straight counterparts. It was Windsor's case that eventually wound up in front of the Supreme Court and led to the federal recognition of same-sex couples in 2013.[5]

When the Supreme Court reached its decision in *Obergefell v. Hodges*, news media interns raced outside to pass information to reporters. Cameras and news crews were not allowed inside when the Supreme Court gave its ruling.

Many of the first states' legalizations of same-sex marriage came through the court systems. Both Massachusetts's and Connecticut's legalization came after the state supreme courts ruled that the bans of individual states violated the rights of same-sex couples within the states. Connecticut legalized same-sex marriage soon after its court's ruling. Massachusetts's ruling allowed same-sex marriages immediately. In 2009, Vermont became the first state to legalize same-sex marriage by legislative vote.

Following the US Supreme Court's ruling on DOMA, many states legalized same-sex marriage. In 2014, only 15 states still held constitutional bans on same-sex marriage. In 2015, when the Supreme Court ruled on *Obergefell v. Hodges*, LGBTQ advocates across the country rejoiced.

RELIGIOUS LIBERTY

At the forefront for opponents of same-sex marriage was and still is the issue of religious liberty. The question was this: Do churches have to perform same-sex marriages even if it goes against their religious beliefs? The short answer is no. The longer answer is a bit more complicated.

In the majority opinion in *Obergefell*, Justice Kennedy made clear that the decision would not impact people whose beliefs denied recognition of same-sex marriages. However, the rights of a citizen can be limited once they start to impact the rights of another citizen. That holds true across all freedoms. One faith cannot infringe on another person's faith.

In 2012, Colorado bakery owner Jack Phillips refused to make

THE SEPARATION OF CHURCH AND STATE

The First Amendment to the US Constitution states, "Congress shall make no law respecting an establishment of religion, or prohibiting the free exercise thereof."[6] There is meant to be a clear separation between church and government, often referred to as the separation of church and state. It is a tricky balance to strike. Legislators must navigate their religious convictions and their jobs as state and national representatives.

a cake for a same-sex couple's wedding. The couple sued, and the case was taken to the Supreme Court in 2018 as *Masterpiece Cakeshop v. Colorado Civil Rights Commission*. Phillips went before the US Supreme Court claiming he did not have to make a cake for a same-sex couple because of his religion. While the court ruled in his favor, it was not because of religious liberty. Instead of citing Phillips's freedom to discriminate against LGBTQ customers, the court went a different route. The Colorado Civil Rights Commission had ordered Phillips to make the cake for a gay couple in 2012. However, in the letter containing the order, one commissioner had called the religious rhetoric "despicable."[7]

The Supreme Court ruled in Jack Phillips's favor. However, it upheld that businesses must provide equal access to all people.

ORDAINING LGBTQ MINISTERS AND FAITH LEADERS

A 2014 survey of lesbian, gay, and bisexual Americans found that almost 50 percent identified as belonging to a Christian religious denomination. An additional 11 percent of respondents identified with another faith, such as Judaism, Buddhism, Hinduism, or Islam.[8] People may associate Christianity with being against LGBTQ rights and people. The majority of Christian and Jewish faith institutions do not accept LGBTQ people and marriage equality. However, many people who practice Christianity and Judaism are accepting of LGBTQ people and marriage equality.

Many of these stances of support have come to light in the last decade. With this support came an important step for many spiritual LGBTQ people: the possibility of ordination. Living openly as LGBTQ as a pastor, minister, or rabbi can have a huge impact on a person's ability to serve their congregation fully. In 2016, 111 clergy members from the United Methodist Church signed a letter coming out, stating their sexuality and gender identity.[9] The letter went on to say that it was impossible for LGBTQ clergy to serve their communities effectively if a significant part of themselves had to remain hidden.

As of 2015, eight major religious organizations in the United States sanctioned same-sex marriages.[10] Of those, all allowed the ordination of LGB clergy, and most allowed the ordination of transgender clergy.

Karen Oliveto became the first openly lesbian Methodist bishop in 2016.

KIM DAVIS

Kim Davis, a county clerk in Kentucky, came under fire in 2015 after refusing to issue marriage licenses to same-sex couples. Despite the Supreme Court ruling in *Obergefell*, Davis would not comply, citing religious freedom. As a private citizen, Davis has a right to exercise her religion. However, as a public elected official, Davis's claim to religious exemption is not valid. She was voted into her office to uphold the Constitution and the laws of Kentucky. The laws of Kentucky now allowed same-sex marriages. In September 2015, Davis was arrested. She was held in contempt of court—meaning she had failed to do what a court ordered—when she continued to refuse to issue marriage licenses to same-sex couples. Davis lost her reelection bid in the 2018 midterm election.

Because of this, Phillips was denied a neutral decision maker. The Supreme Court ruled in his favor because he was mistreated by government officials. It did not rule in favor of the discrimination.

In *Obergefell v. Hodges*, the majority opinion said that religious liberty would not be affected. However, the dissenting opinion believed each state should have decided for itself whether same-sex marriage was a legal right. In his opinion, Chief Justice Roberts equated marriage with the religious ceremony. Marriages between people of many different religions often involve a religious ceremony. The denomination (or lack of one) of a couple has no bearing over whether the federal government recognizes the marriage.

Still, these fears have made an impact on state legislators, who have created laws that allow private institutions to refuse service to LGBTQ people. Many of these laws were passed in the immediate aftermath of *Obergefell v. Hodges*. In Mississippi, the state legislature passed a law in 2016 called the "Protecting Freedom of Conscience from Government Discrimination Act." Supporters of the law say it protects business owners and people with sincere beliefs.

The law allows businesses to refuse to provide marriage-related services to same-sex couples. Additionally, court magistrates, justices, and other officials are allowed to refuse to perform same-sex marriages. A federal judge in Mississippi claimed that the law allowed "arbitrary discrimination" against LGBTQ people.[11] Such laws may lead other individuals to refuse service to LGBTQ people.

DISCUSSION STARTERS

- Can you think of some instances in which you are not allowed to do something? Why do those rules exist? Can you think of any instance where you felt your rights were being taken away because of those rules?

- What role do you think religion should play in politics? Explain your answer.

- How do you think DOMA impacted the fight for marriage equality? Do you think the United States would have legalized same-sex marriage sooner? Why or why not?

Some same-sex couples want to make a family, though there are still barriers in place after achieving marriage equality.

ADOPTION AND FAMILY PLANNING

A fter *Obergefell*, many assumed that same-sex couples would be able to do everything that opposite-sex couples could do. However, that has not been the case for many LGBTQ couples across the United States who want to make a family. Many barriers exist. According to the American Civil Liberties Union (ACLU), "21 states have granted second-parent adoptions to lesbian and gay couples."[1] In states that do not have second-parent adoptions, those children legally have only one parent. Further, many still have restrictions for gay and lesbian parents to adopt through state-run agencies.

Some conservative organizations make the claim that children thrive best in a household with both a mother and a father. They say LGBTQ parents are putting a political agenda ahead of a child's well-being. Their stance is that mothers and fathers

ADOPTION PAPERS AND SECOND-PARENT ADOPTIONS

A 1977 Florida law stated, "No person . . . may adopt if that person is a homosexual."[3] In 2010, Florida courts ruled that the ban on adoption for gay people was unconstitutional. Despite the 2010 court ruling, adopting through the foster system was still challenging. Daniel and Casanova Nurse of Tallahassee, Florida, encountered many roadblocks when adopting their three children. Because Daniel and Casanova were unable to marry in Florida when they adopted their foster kids, Daniel was the only one listed on the adoption papers. The couple had to add Casanova later. Due to legislation at the time, some adoption agencies could choose to refuse the Nurses because of their sexual orientation. Daniel Nurse testified during a legislative session about a bill that would allow private adoption agencies to turn him away. He said, "Love is unconditional. Love is love, and it's what these children deserve."[4]

take care of children differently, and this complementary role of parenting is imperative to the development of a child.

People who oppose adoption by LGBTQ parents state that little research has been done on the outcomes of children raised by LGBTQ couples. Because the data is inconclusive, they say there is no proof LGBTQ couples make good parents. However, Cornell University compiled a collection of 79 studies spanning the years 1980 through 2017 that examined the effects of same-sex parents on children. Of those 79 studies, only four concluded negative outcomes.[2] The four studies with negative outcomes had the same flaw: each sample included children who were raised in a household in which a parent came out as LGBTQ during the child's adolescence, which added stress to the life of the child. This flaw renders the studies scientifically unsound, because any familial disruption, such as a parent leaving for any reason, is known to cause distress for children. This means that the studies do not make a fair comparison between how same-sex parents and opposite-sex parents raise children.

REVISITING RELIGIOUS LIBERTY

In states across the country, legislative leaders are introducing bills called religious liberty bills that serve to protect faith-based adoption and foster organizations. These organizations will receive funding from taxpayers while also discriminating against same-sex couples. Supporters of same-sex adoption fear other repercussions from these decisions will follow. The HRC states that these bills could also impact "interfaith couples, single parents, married couples in which one prospective parent has previously been divorced, or other qualified parents to whom an agency has an objection."[5]

In July 2018, US representative Robert Aderholt of Alabama sponsored an amendment to a bill for the US Departments of Health, Labor, and Education that would allow faith-based adoption and foster agencies to deny service to LGBTQ families for religious reasons. He believed this would lead to a larger number of agencies overall because additional agencies

A 2018 Williams Institute survey found that there were more than 700,000 same-sex couples in the United States. About half of these couples were married. The other half were unmarried but living together. About 16 percent of same-sex couples were raising children. Thirty-nine percent of opposite-sex couples were raising children. However, same-sex couples were significantly more likely to be raising adopted children or fostering. While 21 percent of same-sex parents were raising adopted children, only 3 percent of their opposite-sex peers were doing the same. Similarly, 2.9 percent of same-sex couples were foster parents. Only 0.4 percent of opposite-sex parents fostered. Some foster agencies welcome the diversity that same-sex couples provide.[7]

In 2018, central Florida was facing a shortage of foster homes for kids. In Orange and Osceola counties alone, 1,300 kids were in the state's care. One lesbian couple at first wasn't sure fostering was right for them. But in three years, they've fostered 13 children. Sometimes they've had as many as five kids in their home. Reflecting on the experience, they said, "People say things like 'Thank God for you; I could never do that.' We say, 'Listen, we're the ones getting this gift. These kids come into our home, and each and every one leaves us a special memory in our hearts.'"[8]

would open that catered to LGBTQ clients. Aderholt argued that by providing more agencies, there would be more homes for children. Supporters believe that there will be no effect on the placement of children with LGBTQ people. LGBTQ advocates are not certain this will be the case. They worry that agencies that deny a family based on sexual orientation are also denying children a loving family.

THE RIGHT TO A HOME

There are roughly 10.7 million LGBTQ people in the United States. They account for 4.3 percent of the US population.[6]

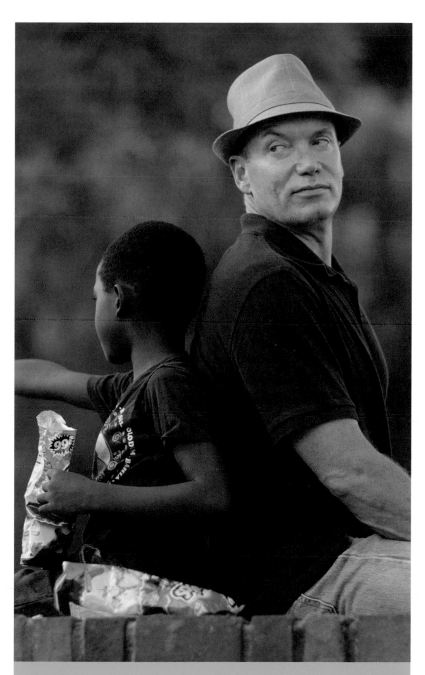

Frank Martin Gill, *right*, pictured with his adopted son, sued the state of Florida in 2010 to overturn a law that banned gays and lesbians from adopting children.

Many of these people choose to raise families regardless of whether they are married. Forty-eight percent of women and 20 percent of men in the LGBTQ community across the United States are raising children under the age of 18.[9] Many of these families are concentrated in the South, Northwest, and Midwest regions of the country. These are also the regions with some of the fewest protections for LGBTQ families who are affected most by religious liberty laws. In these regions, LGBTQ people are more likely to come out later in life. They are more likely to have children from a previous opposite-sex partnership.

The percentage of LGBTQ youth in foster care is higher than the percentage of LGBTQ youth in the general population. Many LGBTQ youth enter the foster system for the same reasons as their non-LGBTQ peers. However, many of them have

A HOME FOR YOUTH

The Lambert House in Seattle, Washington, was the first organization dedicated to LGBTQ youth to receive nonprofit status. Serving Seattle LGBTQ youth since 1981, the Lambert House helps LGBTQ youth feel valued and welcome in their community. The House has more than 70 volunteer community members in addition to paid staff who serve as informal mentors to the youth that come through the doors.[10] In addition to having a library and computers, the Lambert House is often the first stop for LGBTQ youth who find themselves without a home. Youth are able to receive hygiene products as well as get case support and other resources.

undergone the additional trauma of being verbally or physically abused for their sexual orientation or gender identity.

A study conducted in Los Angeles, California, found that one in five children in the Los Angeles foster system is LGBTQ. LGBTQ children are placed in twice as many homes as non-LGBTQ children.[11] LGBTQ youth also face more harassment and mistreatment in their foster homes. A 2015 survey of LGBTQ youth in New York found that 78 percent had been removed or ran away from their foster home due to hostility.[12] That hostility doesn't come only from other foster kids. LGBTQ youth faced mistreatment from foster parents, too.

LGBTQ youth account for 40 percent of the homeless youth in the United States.[13] Agencies and homeless youth projects are trying to work together to find a solution to this issue by providing supportive environments for LGBTQ youth. Ninety-nine percent of people who work with homeless youth say they work with LGBTQ youth.[14]

RESOURCES FOR LGBTQ YOUTH EXPERIENCING HOMELESSNESS

The lack of resources for LGBTQ youth experiencing homelessness exposes many of them to risk factors at much higher rates than their straight peers. LGBTQ youth are more likely to be physically and sexually abused, more likely to engage in sex work, and more likely to suffer from substance abuse than their non-LGBTQ peers.[15] There is little legislation available to help these youth.

LGBTQ youth experiencing homelessness may not have access to safe shelters.

LGBTQ-focused nonprofits such as True Colors Fund provide resources to agencies so that they are better able to work with their LGBTQ youth.

States regulate nondiscrimination policies for foster care. As of 2015, less than half of US states had policies that included sexual orientation or gender identity.[16] While the lack of laws does not legalize abuse, LGBTQ youth in the foster system report being verbally and sexually abused, as well as being kicked out. Many homeless LGBTQ youth choose to stay on the streets instead of seeking shelter with agencies.

One legislative act that works to help homeless youth is the Runaway and Homeless Youth Act. This act allows community organizations to provide temporary shelter and services to homeless and runaway youth. However, this act falls short of the needs of the homeless LGBTQ youth population. Many shelters are located in larger cities. Youth who are in smaller cities and towns have few places to go. More legislation is needed to create additional shelters and resources for youth.

DISCUSSION STARTERS

- What solutions do you see for faith-based adoption agencies that are seeking to exclude same-sex couples? Explain your answer.

- Do you think enough is being done to help homeless LGBTQ youth? What changes would you make, or what resources do you think need to be added for LGBTQ youth?

- How can foster homes create a positive experience for LGBTQ youth?

9

THE FUTURE OF RIGHTS AND LAWS

D espite the significant advancements in equality for LGBTQ people in the United States, there are still many hurdles to overcome. With each election comes new leadership and new ideas on how best to serve all US citizens. Most court cases take years of litigation before they make it to the Supreme Court. Additionally, the Supreme Court hears only approximately 100 cases per year out of some 7,000 applications.[1] Generally, the court only hears cases that it feels are important or interesting.

Electing politicians who support equality is important for the future of LGBTQ Americans. It's important to put diverse voices in Congress and every level of government. Diversity allows empathy and compromise to grow in policy making. Achieving this goal relies on voters to elect these officials.

EMPLOYMENT NONDISCRIMINATION

When the Civil Rights Act was passed in 1964, it prohibited discrimination against people based on race, color, national origin, sex, or religion. Since that time, numerous amendments have expanded the reach of the act. However, the classes of people protected in the act have remained the same. Between 1974 and 2017, seven different pieces of legislation to amend the Civil Rights Act were introduced to Congress to address LGBTQ civil rights. None of them passed. However, the US Commission on Civil Rights released a report in November 2017 outlining the reach and effect of LGBTQ discrimination in the workplace. The report is the first to focus only on LGBTQ civil rights. The findings in this 154-page report renewed a sense of urgency in addressing a widespread issue.[2]

The report cited a statistic that nearly one-half of nonheterosexual employees experienced harassment. For transgender employees that percentage was 90 percent.[3] The commission also recognized that there is little consistency between state laws, leaving LGBTQ employees unprotected. Currently 26 states have no protections in place for sexual orientation, and 28 don't address gender identity and expression.[4] The commission called for immediate action from Congress to pass an antidiscrimination bill for LGBTQ people.

An amendment to the Civil Rights Act, called the Equality Act, was introduced in both the House and Senate in 2017 and is expected to be voted on between 2019 and 2021. Throughout the act, "sexual orientation" and "gender identity" would be added as protected statuses against discrimination in public accommodations.[5] This is an important amendment for LGBTQ rights, not only in the workplace but at concert venues, bakeries, public transit, and public schools and universities. US Commission on Civil Rights chair Catherine Lhamon said the amendment "[fills] in a gap in our civil rights protections."[6]

LGBTQ REPRESENTATION IN AMERICAN POLITICS

The year 2018 saw a rise in the number of LGBTQ people running for political office at the local, state, and national levels. Some people referred to this as the "Rainbow Wave." After the 2018 midterm election, there were eight openly gay, lesbian, or bisexual members elected to Congress.[7] Sharice Davids, a representative from Kansas, was the first lesbian congresswoman from the state as well as one of the first two Native American congresswomen from the entire country. However, there were zero openly trans members of Congress.

State legislatures have also seen a rise in the number of LGBTQ candidates running for office, some in states that have yet to have an LGBTQ representative. The Victory Fund, an LGBTQ advocacy group, reported that in total 154 LGBTQ people were elected to local, state, and federal positions.[8] For example, Colorado governor Jared Polis is the first openly gay governor in any state. Additionally, two trans women—Gerri Cannon and Lisa Bunker—were elected to the New Hampshire House of Representatives.

MAKING CHANGE IN THE LGBTQ COMMUNITY

Social movement organizations such as the Trans Women of Color Collective (TWOCC) are vital to the changing of rights and laws for LGBTQ people across the country. TWOCC prioritizes the voices of transgender women of color. Trans women of color represent the most-targeted population for hate crimes. TWOCC puts those women in positions of power to enact change at the local and national levels. These women speak at universities in the United States to promote understanding and advocacy for LGBTQ people of color. It is their hope and belief that spreading information will create greater empathy across identities. The LGBTQ community is focused on promoting intersectionality. Intersectionality is the consideration of how various parts of someone's identity, such as race, sexual orientation, and gender identity, affect their life. It is important because it impacts the types of laws that advocacy groups demand from legislators. Advocacy groups need to consider what effects legislation will have on all minority populations.

Some of the largest changes in attitudes and laws happen closest to home. Change can and often does happen first at the local and state level. Little changes, put together, can make big impacts. Many states are introducing legislation that protects LGBTQ people inside and outside the workplace. However, with the current political environment, it's not surprising that legislation to limit the freedoms of LGBTQ people is also being introduced. For example, 129 such bills in 30 states were introduced in 2017.[9] Not all of them passed. But a few have already been signed into law by state governors.

For example, the Oklahoma state senate passed a bill that allowed adoption and foster agencies to choose not to place children with LGBTQ couples because of the organizations' religious views. The bill states that LGBTQ couples being turned away is not enough of a reason to change the laws. Such laws discriminate against LGBTQ people but also against other

In July 2018, the Trans-Latinx March raised awareness of the latinx transgender community in Queens, New York. Organizers stated that the purpose of the march was to "[demand] the rights" of the community.

groups, such as unmarried couples, whose status could be viewed by the private agencies to be against their faith.

TRANS INCLUSIVITY

Throughout the struggle for equality within the LGBTQ movement, trans people have been left with far fewer protections than nonheterosexual people. As of 2018, only 17 states and Washington, DC, prohibited insurance companies from excluding trans health-care needs.[10] In states where exclusions can still happen, trans people can be denied coverage for transition-related care including hormones and counseling. However, for people insured under the Affordable Care Act, trans-inclusionary coverage is protected regardless of the state the person lives in.

CHANGING LAWS BY LOOKING BACK

On the largest Navajo reservation in the United States, the history of colonization and assimilation has led LGBTQ Native Americans to face significant stigma and rejection from their tribal leaders. However, many of these people are finding support with their grandparents. One woman, Michelle Sherman, is a lesbian. She now lives with her grandmother on the reservation. She says, "When I came out to my family, they kicked me out, but my grandma told them that this was a normal part of Navajo culture."[11] The elders of the tribe still adhere to old cultural traditions. Now, young people are looking toward their heritage to argue for increased equality on the reservation. They see that equality used to exist. There is hope that laws and rights for Native American LGBTQ people can change with the help of the knowledge from the tribal elders.

As anti-bullying initiatives continue to undergo reform, it will be important to consider trans and gender-nonconforming students in those updates. Trans students are often the most targeted in schools. They feel they have no one who will back them up. GLSEN recommends a comprehensive nondiscrimination and anti-bullying policy for schools in every state. Enacting those policies could be challenging, particularly if the state does not enforce its anti-bullying policies.

The pink and black triangles became symbols of solidarity and a reminder never to go back to the way things once were. Similarly, it is important to remember the history of LGBTQ people in the United States. This is not only to recognize the progress that has been made within the last 100 years but also to serve as a reminder to always seek something better for every person. The laws of the country have a ripple effect on the way people treat each other. It is the hope of every LGBTQ advocate that in the future, laws will be filled with kindness and acceptance instead of discrimination.

DISCUSSION STARTERS

- After reading this book, what do you think is the most important area for lawmakers to focus on for LGBTQ rights? Explain your answer.

- How do all people benefit from a broader understanding of gender and sexuality?

ESSENTIAL FACTS

SIGNIFICANT EVENTS

- Don't Ask, Don't Tell (DADT) was the compromise reached by Congress in 1993. It permitted gay and lesbian soldiers to serve in the military but required them to stay closeted. DADT wasn't repealed until 2010.

- *United States v. Windsor* was the landmark Supreme Court case that overturned the Defense of Marriage Act in 2013.

- In 2015, the Supreme Court delivered its opinion on *Obergefell v. Hodges*. Its ruling legalized marriage equality across the United States.

KEY PLAYERS

- Justice Anthony Kennedy wrote the majority opinions for the Supreme Court for many of the recent major LGBTQ rights cases. He retired from the Supreme Court in 2018.

- CeCe McDonald is a black trans woman. She was arrested for defending herself against an attacker. Now she is an activist. She lectures on trans rights and the criminal justice system.

- Edie Windsor sued the government after the IRS sent her a bill for $300,000 in inheritance taxes. Her case allowed for the federal recognition of married same-sex couples.

IMPACT ON SOCIETY

Many people believed that after the *Obergefell v. Hodges* decision, the LGBTQ rights movement was over. They believed equality had been reached. The Supreme Court decision that led to marriage equality was a huge step. However, there are still discriminatory laws and practices in the United States. There are no federal nondiscrimination policies for LGBTQ Americans. As of January 2019, trans people are excluded from serving in the military, and lawsuits challenging this ban are still being considered. Adoption and foster care policies are not consistent from state to state. Some places have many protections for LGBTQ people. Others have very few. Until equality stretches across the whole country, the American LGBTQ rights movement will not be finished.

QUOTE

"We have lives. We have people who love us. We need the same opportunities in life to survive and to live and to thrive."

—*CeCe McDonald*

GLOSSARY

AUTONOMY
The idea that a person has control and agency over their body.

CLAUSE
A section of a bill or amendment.

COMMUNISM
A political system in which the government controls the economy and owns all property.

CONSENSUAL
Done with permission.

DISSENT
To express a different opinion from others.

DRAG QUEEN
A performer, usually a cisgender man, who dresses as a woman for the purpose of entertaining others at bars, clubs, or other events.

INJUNCTION
An order from a court meant to stop or prevent an activity found by the court to be unlawful.

LITIGATION
The process of taking legal action.

NONBINARY
Having a gender identity that is neither male nor female, or sometimes both male and female.

ORDAIN

In religion, to allow a person to become a clergy member of a church or synagogue.

PERVERSION

Bad morals, especially in relation to sexual practices.

PETITIONER

Someone who is suing another person or organization.

PRECEDENT

In court cases, a ruling on a case that serves as a guide for future related rulings.

REPERCUSSION

A consequence for an action or law.

RESPONDENT

In a Supreme Court case, a person arguing the law is constitutional.

SUSCEPTIBLE

Open to an influence such as an ideology.

ADDITIONAL RESOURCES

SELECTED BIBLIOGRAPHY

Davis, Heath Fogg. *Beyond Trans: Does Gender Matter?* New York UP, 2017.

Gleason, James. "LGBT History: The Lavender Scare." *National LGBT Chamber of Commerce*, 3 Oct. 2017, nglcc.org. Accessed 12 Nov. 2018.

"Two-Spirit." *Indian Health Services*, n.d., ihs.gov. Accessed 12 Nov. 2018.

Waxman, Olivia B. "How the Nazi Regime's Pink Triangle Symbol Was Repurposed for LGBTQ Pride." *Time*, 31 May 2018, time.com. Accessed 12 Nov. 2018.

FURTHER READINGS

Decker, Julie Sondra. *The Invisible Orientation*. Skyhorse Publishing, 2015.

Harris, Duchess and Kristin Marciniak. *LGBTQ Discrimination in America*. Abdo, 2020.

Poehlmann, Tristan. *The Stonewall Riots: The Fight for LGBT Rights*. Abdo, 2017.

ONLINE RESOURCES

Booklinks
NONFICTION NETWORK
FREE! ONLINE NONFICTION RESOURCES

To learn more about LGBTQ rights and the law, please visit **abdobooklinks.com** or scan this QR code. These links are routinely monitored and updated to provide the most current information available.

MORE INFORMATION

For more information on this subject, contact or visit the following organizations:

GLSEN
110 William St., Thirtieth Floor
New York, NY 10038
glsen.org

GLSEN is an advocate for LGBTQ students in the United States. They have resources for schools to be more welcoming and supportive of students.

HUMAN RIGHTS CAMPAIGN
1640 Rhode Island Ave. NW
Washington, DC 20036
hrc.org

The Human Rights Campaign (HRC) is an advocacy group and civil rights organization for LGBTQ people.

STONEWALL NATIONAL MONUMENT
Intersection of Christopher, Grove, and Fourth Sts.
New York, NY 10014
nps.gov/ston/index.htm

The Stonewall National Monument is the first national monument dedicated to LGBTQ people and the fight for civil rights.

SOURCE NOTES

CHAPTER 1. "A LITTLE MORE PERFECT"

1. Barack Obama. "Remarks by the President on the Supreme Court Decision on Marriage Equality." *White House*, 26 June 2015, obamawhitehouse.archives.gov. Accessed 7 Dec. 2018.

2. Adam Liptak. "Supreme Court Ruling Makes Same-Sex Marriage a Right Nationwide." *New York Times*, 26 June 2015, nytimes.com. Accessed 7 Dec. 2018.

3. United States Supreme Court. *Obergefell v. Hodges*. Opinions of the Court—2014, Supreme Court, 26 June 2015, supremecourt.gov. Accessed 7 Dec. 2018.

4. "Due Process." *Wex*, n.d., law.cornell.edu/wex. Accessed 7 Dec. 2018.

5. Bella DePaulo. "Know Your 1,138 Marital Privileges, Courtesy of the Feds." *HuffPost*, 29 June 2010, huffingtonpost.com. Accessed 7 Dec. 2018.

6. Donald Verrilli Jr. "Obergefell v. Hodges," *Supreme Court of the United States*, n.d., supremecourt.gov. Accessed 7 Dec. 2018.

7. United States Supreme Court. *Obergefell v. Hodges*.

8. Jeffrey M. Jones. "In U.S., 10.2% of LGBT Adults Now Married to Same-Sex Spouse." *Gallup*, 22 June 2017, news.gallup.com. Accessed 7 Dec. 2018.

9. David Masci, Anna Brown, and Jocelyn Kiley. "5 Facts about Same-Sex Marriage." *Pew Research Center*, 26 June 2017, pewresearch.org. Accessed 7 Dec. 2018.

10. Michael S. Rosenwald. "How Jim Obergefell Became the Face of the Gay Marriage Case." *Washington Post*, 6 Apr. 2015, washingtonpost.com. Accessed 7 Dec. 2018.

CHAPTER 2. WORKPLACE DISCRIMINATION

1. "2017 Workplace Equality Fact Sheet." *Out and Equal Workplace Advocates*, n.d., outandequal.org. Accessed 7 Dec. 2018.

2. Judith Adkins. "Congressional Investigations and the Lavender Scare." *Prologue Magazine*, 2016, archives.gov. Accessed 7 Dec. 2018.

3. "2015 U.S. Transgender Survey Executive Summary," *National Center for Transgender Equality*, Dec. 2016, transequality.org. Accessed 7 Dec. 2018.

4. "Equality Maps: State Non-Discrimination Laws." *Movement Advancement Project*, 3 Dec. 2018, lgbtmap.org. Accessed 7 Dec. 2018.

5. John Paul Brammer. "Jury Awards Transgender Professor $1.1 Million in Discrimination Case." *NBC News*, 20 Nov. 2017, nbcnews.com. Accessed 7 Dec. 2018.

6. Toni G. Atkins. "It's Time to End Discrimination in the Workplace." *HuffPost*, 12 June 2016, huffingtonpost.com. Accessed 7 Jan. 2019.

7. "2017 Workplace Equality Fact Sheet."

8. "2017 Workplace Equality Fact Sheet."

9. "2017 Workplace Equality Fact Sheet."

CHAPTER 3. HEALTH AND PRIVACY

1. "Genesis 19:1–28." *New International Version*. Biblica, 2011. *BibleGateway.com*, biblegateway.com. Accessed 10 Dec. 2018.

2. "Genesis 19:1–28."

3. Melvin I. Urofsky. "Lawrence v. Texas." *Encyclopaedia Britannica*, 27 Sept. 2018, britannica.com. Accessed 10 Dec. 2018.

4. Urofsky, "Lawrence v. Texas."

5. Rictor Norton. "A Critique of Social Constructionism and Postmodern Queer Theory," *Gay History and Literature*, 19 June 2008, rictornorton.co.uk. Accessed 10 Dec. 2018.

6. Jamie Scot. "Shock the Gay Away: Secrets of Early Gay Aversion Therapy Revealed (Photos)." *HuffPost*, 6 Dec. 2017, huffingtonpost.com. Accessed 10 Dec. 2018.

7. "Community," *AVENwiki*, 19 Aug. 2017, wiki.asexuality.org. Accessed 10 Dec. 2018.

CHAPTER 4. SAFE SCHOOLS AND STUDENTS' RIGHTS

1. "Report Examines Anti-Bullying Policies." *GLSEN*, 15 July 2015, glsen.org. Accessed 10 Dec. 2018.

2. "2011 National School Climate Survey." *GLSEN*, 5 Sept. 2012, glsen.org. Accessed 10 Dec. 2018.

3. Stephen Peters. "LGBT Youth Deserve to Learn in Environments Free from Harassment and Bullying." *Human Rights Campaign*, 29 Jan. 2015, hrc.org. Accessed 10 Dec. 2018.

4. Erin M. Sullivan et al. "Suicide Trends among Persons Aged 10–24 Years—United States, 1994–2012." *Centers for Disease Control and Prevention*, 6 Mar. 2015, cdc.gov. Accessed 10 Dec. 2018.

5. "Facts about Suicide." *Trevor Project*, n.d., thetrevorproject.org. Accessed 10 Dec. 2018.

6. Movement Advancement Project. *LGBT Policy Spotlight: Conversion Therapy Bans*, July 2017, lgbtmap.org. Accessed 10 Dec. 2018.

7. Rokia Hassanein. "New Study Reveals Shocking Rates of Attempted Suicide among Trans Adolescents." *Human Rights Campaign*, 12 Sept. 2018, hrc.org. Accessed 10 Dec. 2018.

8. "2015 National School Climate Survey." *GLSEN*, 2016, glsen.org. Accessed 10 Dec. 2018.

9. Zack Ford. "Exclusive: Mother of Transgender Daughter Kept Out of Locker Room during Lockdown Drill Speaks Out." *ThinkProgress*, 11 Oct. 2018, thinkprogress.org. Accessed 10 Dec. 2018.

10. Cory Turner and Anya Kamenetz. "The Education Department Says It Won't Act on Transgender Student Bathroom Access." *NPR*, 12 Feb. 2018, npr.org. Accessed 10 Dec. 2018.

11. Moriah Balingit. "Education Department No Longer Investigating Transgender Bathroom Complaints." *Washington Post*, 12 Feb. 2018, washingtonpost.com. Accessed 10 Dec. 2018.

12. "The Experience of LGBT Students in School Athletics." *GLSEN*, 2013, glsen.org. Accessed 10 Dec. 2018.

13. "2015 National School Climate Survey."

14. "'No Promo Homo' Laws." *GLSEN*, n.d., glsen.org. Accessed 10 Dec. 2018.

15. Corinne Segal. "Eight States Censor LGBTQ Topics in School. Now, a Lawsuit Is Challenging That." *PBS*, 29 Jan. 2017, pbs.org. Accessed 10 Dec. 2018.

16. Office of Adolescent Health. "Trends in Teen Pregnancy and Childbearing." *US Department of Health and Human Services*, 2 June 2016, hhs.gov. Accessed 10 Dec. 2018.

CHAPTER 5. LOST IN TRANSLATION

1. "The New Science of Sex and Gender." *Scientific American*, 1 Sept. 2017, scientificamerican.com. Accessed 10 Dec. 2018.

2. Human Rights Watch and interACT. "'I Want to Be Like Nature Made Me.'" *Human Rights Watch*, 25 Jul. 2017, hrw.org. Accessed 10 Dec. 2018.

3. Duane Brayboy. "Two Spirits, One Heart, Five Genders." *Indian Country Today*, 7 Sept. 2017, newsmaven.io. Accessed 10 Dec. 2018.

4. Rebecca Nagle. "The Healing History of Two-Spirit, a Term That Gives LGBTQ Natives a Voice." *HuffPost*, 30 June 2018, huffingtonpost.com. Accessed 10 Dec. 2018.

5. Brayboy, "Two Spirits."

6. "Arresting Dress." *PBS News Hour*, 31 May 2015, pbs.org. Accessed 10 Dec. 2018.

7. "Stonewall Riots." *Encyclopaedia Britannica*, 21 June 2018, britannica.com. Accessed 10 Dec. 2018.

8. J. Hirby. "How Much Does It Cost to Change Your Name?" *Law Dictionary*, n.d., thelawdictionary.org. Accessed 10 Dec. 2018.

9. Bureau of Consular Affairs. "Change of Sex Marker." *US Department of State*, n.d., travel.state.gov. Accessed 10 Dec. 2018.

10. Simon Briggs. "Why Tennis's Renée Richards, the First Transgender Woman to Play Professional Sport, Matters Today." *Telegraph*, 30 Mar. 2018, telegraph.co.uk. Accessed 10 Dec. 2018.

11. Samantha Cowan. "Laverne Cox and CeCe McDonald Discuss the Epidemic of Violence against Trans Women." *Takepart*, 3 June 2016, takepart.com. Accessed 10 Dec. 2018.

SOURCE NOTES
CONTINUED

CHAPTER 6. LIFE IN THE MILITARY

1. Catherine S. Manegold. "The Odd Place of Homosexuality in the Military." *New York Times*, 18 Apr. 1993, nytimes.com. Accessed 11 Dec. 2018.

2. Sarah Pruitt. "Was 'Don't Ask, Don't Tell' a Step Forward for LGBT in the Military?" *History*, 25 Apr. 2018, history.com. Accessed 11 Dec. 2018.

3. Chloe Hadjimatheou. "Christine Jorgensen: 60 Years of Sex Change Ops." *BBC News*, 30 Nov. 2012, bbc.com. Accessed 11 Dec. 2018.

4. Olivia B. Waxman. "How the Nazi Regime's Pink Triangle Symbol Was Repurposed for LGBTQ Pride." *Time*, 31 May 2018, time.com. Accessed 11 Dec. 2018.

5. Lily Rothman. "How a Closeted Air Force Sergeant Became the Face of Gay Rights." *Time*, 8 Sept. 2015, time.com. Accessed 11 Dec. 2018.

6. Pruitt, "Was 'Don't Ask, Don't Tell' a Step Forward?"

7. CBS News. "Abuse of Gays in Military Increases." *CBS News*, 9 Mar. 2000, cbsnews.com. Accessed 11 Dec. 2018.

8. Stephanie Russell-Kraft. "'Don't Ask, Don't Tell' Is Gone, but Its Effects Still Haunt LGBT Veterans." *Task & Purpose*, 28 Feb. 2018, taskandpurpose.com. Accessed 11 Dec. 2018.

9. Pruitt, "Was 'Don't Ask, Don't Tell' a Step Forward?"

10. Richard Wolf. "Supreme Court Allows Trump's Partial Military Ban on Transgender People in Military to Take Effect." *USA Today*, 22 Jan. 2019, usatoday.com. Accessed 22 Jan. 2019.

11. Jeremy Diamond. "Trump to Reinstate US Military Ban on Transgender People." *CNN*, 26 Jul. 2017, cnn.com. Accessed 11 Dec. 2018.

CHAPTER 7. THE FIGHT FOR MARRIAGE EQUALITY

1. Richard Socarides. "Why Bill Clinton Signed the Defense of Marriage Act." *New Yorker*, 8 Mar. 2013, newyorker.com. Accessed 11 Dec. 2018.

2. "H.R. 3396 (104th): Defense of Marriage Act." *Gov Track*, n.d., govtrack.us. Accessed 11 Dec. 2018.

3. Bill Clinton. "Bill Clinton: It's Time to Overturn DOMA." *Washington Post*, 7 Mar. 2013, washingtonpost.com. Accessed 11 Dec. 2018.

4. "Changing Attitudes on Gay Marriage." *Pew Research Center*, 26 June 2017, pewforum.org. Accessed 11 Dec. 2018.

5. Robert D. McFadden. "Edith Windsor, Whose Same-Sex Marriage Fight Led to Landmark Ruling, Dies at 88." *New York Times*, 12 Sept. 2017, nytimes.com. Accessed 11 Dec. 2018.

6. "First Amendment." *Legal Information Institute*, n.d., law.cornell.edu. Accessed 11 Dec. 2018.

7. CPR News Staff and the Associated Press. "Former Civil Rights Commissioner Diann Rice Speaks Out: 'I Don't Have Any Regrets.'" *Colorado Public Radio*, 6 June 2018, cpr.org. Accessed 11 Dec. 2018.

8. Eliel Cruz. "Report: Half of LGB Americans Identify as Christian." *Advocate*, 12 May 2015, advocate.com. Accessed 11 Dec. 2018.

9. Daniel Burke. "Defying Church Ban, Dozens of Methodist Clergy Come Out as Gay and Lesbian." *CNN*, 9 May 2016, cnn.com. Accessed 11 Dec. 2018.

10. David Masci and Michael Lipka. "Where Christian Churches, Other Religions Stand on Gay Marriage." *Pew Research Center*, 21 Dec. 2015, pewresearch.org. Accessed 11 Dec. 2018.

11. Lawrence Hurley. "Supreme Court Won't Hear Challenge to Mississippi Anti-LGBT 'Religious Freedom' Law." *PRI*, 8 Jan 2018, pri.org. Accessed 11 Dec. 2018.

CHAPTER 8. ADOPTION AND FAMILY PLANNING

1. "Overview of Lesbian and Gay Parenting, Adoption, and Foster Care." *ACLU*, n.d., aclu.org. Accessed 11 Dec. 2018.

2. "What Does the Scholarly Research Say about the Well-Being of Children with Gay or Lesbian Parents?" *What We Know: The Public Policy Research Portal*, n.d., whatweknow.inequality.cornell.edu. Accessed 11 Dec. 2018.

3. Ronni L. Santo. *Unheard Voices*. Greenwood, 1999. 14.

4. Rebecca Beitsch. "Despite Same-Sex Marriage Ruling, Gay Adoption Rights Uncertain in Some States." *Pew Trusts*, 19 Aug. 2015, pewtrusts.org. Accessed 11 Dec. 2018.

5. Nick Morrow. "Breaking: House Appropriations Republicans Adopt 'License to Discriminate' Amendment." *Human Rights Campaign*, 11 July 2018, hrc.org. Accessed 11 Dec. 2018.

6. "LGBTQ Family Fact Sheet." *Family Equality Council*, n.d., familyequality.org. Accessed 11 Dec. 2018.

7. Shoshana K. Goldberg and Kerith J. Conron. "How Many Same-Sex Couples in the U.S. Are Raising Children?" *Williams Institute UCLA School of Law*, July 2018, williamsinstitute.law.ucla.edu. Accessed 11 Dec. 2018.

8. Kate Santich. "Single Parents, Same-Sex Couples Recruited in 'Critical' Need for Foster Homes in Central Florida." *Orlando Sentinel*, 16 Apr. 2018, orlandosentinel.com. Accessed 11 Dec. 2018.

9. "LGBTQ Family Fact Sheet."

10. "Our History." *Lambert House*, n.d., lamberthouse.org. Accessed 11 Dec. 2018.

11. "LGBTQ Youth in the Foster Care System." *Human Rights Campaign*, n.d., hrc.org. Accessed 11 Dec. 2018.

12. "LGBTQ Youth in the Foster Care System."

13. "Our Issue." *True Colors Fund*, n.d., truecolorsfund.org. Accessed 11 Dec. 2018.

14. "Our Issue."

15. "LGBTQ Youth in the Foster Care System."

16. "LGBTQ Youth in the Foster Care System."

CHAPTER 9. THE FUTURE OF RIGHTS AND LAWS

1. Joseph P. Williams. "How a Case Gets Heard by the Supreme Court." *US News*, 12 Jan. 2017, usnews.com. Accessed 11 Dec. 2018.

2. Williams, "How a Case Gets Heard."

3. "Equality Maps: State Non-Discrimination Laws."

4. "Equality Maps: State Non-Discrimination Laws."

5. "H.R. 2282—115th Congress (2017–2018)." *U.S. Congress*, 2 June 2017, congress.gov. Accessed 11 Dec. 2018.

6. "H.R. 2282."

7. "A Rainbow Wave of Historic Victories for LGBTQ Candidates." *Victory Fund*, 8 Nov. 2018, victoryfund.org. Accessed 11 Dec. 2018.

8. "A Rainbow Wave of Historic Victories."

9. Julie Moreau. "129 Anti-LGBTQ State Bills Were Introduced in 2017, New Report Says." *NBC News*, 12 Jan. 2018, nbcnews.com. Accessed 11 Dec. 2018.

10. "State Maps of Laws and Policies: Transgender Healthcare." *Human Rights Campaign*, 29 Mar. 2018, hrc.org. Accessed 11 Dec. 2018.

11. Jeremy Meek. "Photos of Queer Life on a Sprawling Native American Reservation." *Broadly*, 14 Nov. 2017, broadly.vice.com. Accessed 11 Dec. 2018.

INDEX

ABOUT THE AUTHORS

DUCHESS HARRIS, JD, PHD

Dr. Harris is a professor of American Studies at Macalester College and curator of the Duchess Harris Collection of ABDO books. She is also the coauthor of the titles in the collection, which features popular selections such as *Hidden Human Computers: The Black Women of NASA* and series including News Literacy and Being Female in America.

Before working with ABDO, Dr. Harris authored several other books on the topics of race, culture, and American history. She served as an associate editor for *Litigation News*, the American Bar Association Section of Litigation's quarterly flagship publication, and was the first editor in chief of *Law Raza*, an interactive online journal covering race and the law, published at William Mitchell College of Law. She has earned a PhD in American Studies from the University of Minnesota and a JD from William Mitchell College of Law.

MARTHA LUNDIN

Martha Lundin graduated with a Master of Fine Arts in Creative Writing from the University of North Carolina Wilmington in 2017. They now live and work in Minnesota.